The Shadow Side
of Community and
the Growth of the Self

The Shadow Side
of Community and
the Growth of the Self

Mary Wolff-Salin

CROSSROAD · NEW YORK

1988

The Crossroad Publishing Company
370 Lexington Avenue, New York, N.Y. 10017

Printed in the United States of America

Library of Congress Cataloging-in-Publication Data

Wolff-Salin, Mary.
  The shadow side of community and the growth of the self / Mary
Wolff-Salin.
    p.   cm.
  ISBN 0-8245-0872-6
  1. Monastic and religious life—Psychology. 2. Interpersonal
relations. I. Title.
BX2440.W65   1988
255′.001′9—dc19
                                                        88-11997
                                                             CIP

To the Magazine Street Community,
. . . non loquendo sed vivendo . . .

CONTENTS

INTRODUCTION

I had no intention of writing this book. Another project that seemed (and seems) to me far more appealing was already on the way to being born when I spent a sunny summer afternoon sitting outside with a new friend, one well acquainted with the vicissitudes of community living, notably in religious communities. We talked at great length, wondering why there were so many problems and so much pain; wondering why—to so many— the experience of community was not more invigorating; wondering why solutions were so hard to find. After the conversation, I found myself reflecting on other communities I knew—marriages, families, groups of various kinds. And I reflected on the problems and questions that arose within them. It began to seem important—simply for my own sake—to sort out some of the questions, to ask them, and then to see if any solutions came. Part of this sorting out was listening to other people's questions and pain, as well as their positive experiences. Many of us seek a reason for what so many of us are living through: marriages break up, families dissolve, people leave religious communities— often after years of hard work together. What is it all about?

This book is simply a reflection on community living and an investigation of some of its problems. Most of it is based on people's experience rather than on reading and research. Although much has been written on community in the fields of sociology, anthropology, and psychology, my purpose has been to reflect on all this in only a few chapters and to deal instead with cases, with experience.

The use of case material needs explanation. Case material is usually modified to disguise the identity of the people involved. I have done more, as I have also combined several cases to form a composite. As a result, the case studies here are more "creations" than anything else, with a few exceptions taken from reading or from a well-known, and positive, situation. Hence if any case seems recognizable, that is because of its element of universality, not because the reader truly knows the people involved. Each case needs to be seen as a piece in a mosaic, a movement toward understanding the wider field.

I begin this book with a study of religious community, both in its history and in some contemporary case material. One reason for this choice of subject is that religious communities can in some ways be seen as paradigms of community in general. While some issues can arise in any human community, other issues are different in religious communities, and others—for example, celibacy, family questions, the presence or absence of ideological bases—cause variations in ways of living together. Nonetheless, religious community is a good test-tube situation with which to start. Another reason for this choice is that much of my own experience has been heavily weighted in this direction. I have lived and known religious community in many of its expressions, and it seemed a good thing to explore with some thoroughness. This exploration can certainly be of interest for many nonreligious as well, for the questions of religious community are those of human community. There are, for example, the same questions of relationship and its vicissitudes, the same temptations to withdraw and escape from conflict, the same struggles to work through to a satisfactory situation, the same attempts at control, and the same issues around guilt, ideals, and so many other familiar human experiences. A nun friend of mine who works in a marriage tribunal responded when she was asked what she knew about marriage: "The main issues are less about sex than about relationship, and who should know better than we who live in community what those struggles are?"

The second part of this book deals with a wider field of community and with some heavier material. Cases from marriages, tribal structures, and a therapeutic community are among the examples discussed. Some of these examples come from other books, but only when the experiences seems to have a wider significance than just that one case. Only after these chapters and their listening to what people live through and experience will there be an attempt to draw the threads together with some theoretical reflection and conclusions. As a reading plan for different groups, then, I would suggest that those primarily interested in religious community read part 1 and then, if they wish to keep to lighter work, skip to chapter 12 and the Conclusions. If they feel that these latter come as a quantum leap after part 1, they may want to pick up a few threads in between—perhaps from conclusions of each chapter. For people wanting more in-depth reflection on community, with less stress on religious life, the only shortcut I can tentatively suggest is the omission of chapter 1. The history of religious community may interest them less. Chapters 1, 2, 13, and 14 are the heaviest reading and can be omitted for those who find them indigestible, though the Conclusions may seem to lack basis without them. Once again, the summaries at the end of each chapter may help deal with this problem. Basically, each part of the book is heavier than the last— part 3 most of all. But in the last analysis, the book is simply a reflection on experience. Dipping into that record of experience wherever one wishes is always possible.

Many of the chapters close with a fairy tale, dream, or story. This choice is deliberate. Our daily experiences have symbolic content and meaning. A person who can truly "get under my skin" has that ability because of something in me that can be thus caught—and that something can often be best described in symbolic terms as much as in terms of my history. Legends and fairy tales survive over the years because of the universal and symbolic significance that makes them important in our understanding of ourselves, others, and often human life in general. They are important in therapeutic experience. Oedipus, Cinderella, the Sleeping Beauty, and so many others come to mind. At times, the more universal meaning of a local or "case" situation emerges only when it is placed in such symbolic terms.

This book is addressed to everyone who struggles with questions about community: people in religious communities; people in other forms of community living (families and marriages included) whose questions on the subject are growing; people interested in anthropological and psychological reflection on this subject tested against concrete experience. I believe one finds answers only by asking questions clearly. It is obvious that there is pain in marriages and in communities, but so often we prefer not to look at it and call it by its name. It is this rather disagreeable task that this book undertakes.

Reflection on instances of pain can be one way toward more light. Many of the cases discussed in this book are negative and painful at first sight; the dreams or fairy tales may seem only slightly related; some of the material is difficult reading because, most important of all, it explores the meaning of *individuation* and the *shadow*. However when we try to repress the negative and painful—personally, by not looking at it; or collectively, by not talking about it—we lose one of our best opportunities for growth. Skeletons in the closet have a way of not staying there— whether they appear openly or hide underground and produce "vibes" people cannot understand. Better to take them out, look at them, make friends with them, name them, and find a different level of integration as a result. This is why the title of this book speaks of "shadow," for all these elements are part of the shadow material in our lives.

What, then, is the individuation mentioned above? Many psychological theories use the term—from those which speak of the child's need, once sufficiently loved, to separate from its mother to those which use the more Jungian approach studied in our second chapter.

I use the term in a very specific sense. This book begins by looking at the shadow side of community—the elements of pain, conflict, and brokenness that all of us know to some extent, in community and elsewhere—because I believe that it is precisely out of suffering and death, out of facing, working with, and dealing with these elements that life can emerge. Life does not emerge in the same way when suffering is denied, hidden, or resented. But to face suffering and to work with it as best one can (and the "work" can be just suffering: older spiritual writers spoke of *pati divina*) can transform a person and a life. Individuation in this sense is not reached cheaply or easily, though some people seem to have much more to suffer than others. Nor is this thesis a glorification of pain, for pain can destroy as well as transform. To deal with pain is to deal with fire—a major source of light and warmth, and a possible source of destruction. To speak of individuation is to speak of the constructive and transforming use of this fire—for an individual, a marriage, or a group. The greatest thing one can do for such a communion is what one oneself becomes—for in this becoming something greater than the purely personal self is involved and active. Some of the cases that follow will show this clearly.

Finally, as an introduction to the meaning and importance of community and to make the experience concrete as a human phenomenon, I would like to cite the experience of a friend of mine, of a group that travelled with her, of a writer, and of my own first contact with a monastic community living a quite solitary life in the desert. The reason for this choice is that such a situation can seem to be community at its most esoteric. But because community is about people, it should soon be clear that such is not the case.

My friend was part of a small group of people from a nearby conference center who went out into the desert to see the monastery in question and its life. The group found, first of all, adobe houses in a canyon, miles into a "national wilderness" and away from decent roads. A sign on the gate requested that cars not enter. Near the gate was a guest house and shop; a quarter of a mile down the road was a chapel with a sign instructing people who wished to speak to a monk to ring the bell. Deep silence and the sound of crickets and birds was all one heard. The group went into the chapel and sat down to meditate, hoping that eventually the monks would invite them to dinner. This occurred, and they shared in a silent, simple meal accompanied by reading and followed by an office—the chanting of psalms.

What is the life into which this group came? That of a group of men who arise before four o'clock in the morning to pray and chant psalms in a dark church until the light appears over the canyon, who then go on through a daily rhythm of manual work, reading, study, and prayer, interspersed with meals, household tasks, and the ordinary actions of daily life. There is much silence, notably in the church, refectory, and some other places, but there is sharing, too, as well as meetings (called "chapter"), walks, some exchanges at work or individual conversations. Just the process of living, working, and praying together comes to be a deep sharing in which there is conflict as well as joy. Differences arise;

choices must be made. The group, like all groups, lives by working with these events. And, as in every house, there is cooking, washing, and cleaning to be done; there is work and relaxation, effort and rest. Materially, the life of these men is very ordinary. Guests share in much of their experience.

In *Living Together Alone*, Charles A. Fracchia speaks of a conversation with one member of his community who chose to come there because of his desire for a "communally oriented religious life."[1] The brother comments," . . . what developed was that I got a clearer idea of what I wanted in monastic life: a smaller community and a community in which the members would support each other in living their vocations."[2] Another monk, after speaking of the effort of the group to follow strictly the Benedictine Rule, adds, "But our emphasis is on community life, the relationships of the monks one to another, and an emphasis on the superior . . . being our spiritual father rather than the chief administrator."[3] Despite the silence, then, this group sought a certain togetherness that is of the essence of community living. They wanted mutual support to live their chosen life.

European monastic communities of the same kind of contemplative thrust tend to speak more of solitude and readiness to live alone with God. Yet, paradoxically, one often experiences in just such groups, even many which stress solitude, a level of sharing and community living that less "solitary" groups can envy. When there are difficulties, of course, these reverberate in proportion to this closeness, at least until people learn how to deal with the issue. Fracchia writes:

> Paradoxically, as an increasing number of monastic foundations
> . . . seek a life more attuned to that of St. Benedict's *Rule,* their
> attraction becomes greater. Priests, nuns, and the Catholic laity
> [and, I could add, many non-Catholics of many different faiths
> or lacks of faith] have flocked in growing numbers to monasteries
> for spiritual invigoration. Their experience in these communities
> has not been that of a traditional retreat . . . but a participation
> in the ordinary life of prayer and work led by the monks.[4]

He connects this with a growing desire, among many people, "for more meaningful community life." Certainly, I suspect the group from the conference center went partly out of interest in just such an experience.

In his book Fracchia records a day in the life of this community, from its beginning prayer through the common meal or meals (some days there is only one) and work to the final (eighth) period of common prayer before bed at night—a schedule or "horarium" the guests share with the monks. He watches the alternation between prayer and work; between solitude and togetherness. The monks are not rigid about silence, notably when they work with the guests. However, they do not usually "chat." Their way of life is more serious in its commitment to prayer and the God-seeking life than that. But the hospitality that allows them to share this life with others is part of their commitment, though it is lived in a way that enables them to live their own choice radically as well.

This whole experience had a profound impact on my friend—as on others I have met there. Why? The striking setting and beauty of the site certainly play a part, as does the "differentness" of the life in most externals. Yet here, too, there is a universality that is another part of the attraction. Almost every human being works around the house and in order to earn a living. Many people try to pray and seek God. Most people live with others. What they find in a community like this one is a certain unified way of doing all these things—a certain integration and therefore peace. (The Hebrew term for *peace* in Scripture has to do with integration.) And the unification is not just interior: this life together decade after decade can bring a profound unity, with one another as well as with God. Some of this is also part of what people sense and seek. Perhaps it has to do with some people's dream of what community is about—a dream that, as we noted, some of these monks expressed. A common seeking, a mutual support, a concern with relationship—less as an end in itself and still less as a means than as a strengthening factor in the journey of life—all these have to do with the human experience of community, its difficulties as well as its joys.

People sense in a place like the above an experience that can mean something for the way they also live. And this book wishes to explore some of the pitfalls on this road and some of the challenges they imply, some of the ways these "shadow" elements can also serve on the journey. For there are no easy solutions or easy paths. But the struggle bears its own fruit—if it is carried on wisely. Reflection on experience and on some basic principles around the question of community living (that is, living together) can help us move toward that wisdom, and the writing of this book was meant to be just such a search. My friend expressed it well: "This drive or need to communicate, to suffer against, and to learn to love surfaces in a myriad of forms." We shall look at and reflect on some of these forms.

There are many people I need to thank for help with this work. Dr. Lionel Corbett helped suggest the title; Dr. June Kounin pointed out some ways to broaden the subject beyond its base in religious life; Dr. and Mrs. Gottfried O. Lang helped suggest appropriate anthropological reading; Mrs. Dorothy Edminster made some thought-provoking remarks that started a whole chain of reflection.

I am grateful to Dr. Daveda Tenenbaum; Sister Mary Gehring, OCD; Father Timothy Joyce, OSB; Sisters Maribeth Tobin, Sheila Hammond, Susan Campell, Lorna Brockett, and Susan Maxwell, RSCJ, for their reading and criticism of parts or all of the manuscript; and to Ms. Pamela Newton Renna for more than one insight I have used after her reflective reading—as well as to Messrs. Michael Leach and Frank Oveis of the Crossroad Publishing Company for their unfailing graciousness and helpfulness. And I owe thanks to everyone who shared dreams, reflections, experiences, and questions on the subject with me and thus stimulated my own. Above all I thank the people—religious, married, single, writers, scholars—who have managed to work through and with the challenge of this way of life and have come to a lived understanding of what it can mean, for those who live it and, above all, for the wider human community in our world.

Part One

Religious Community

·1·

A HISTORY OF RELIGIOUS COMMUNITY IN THE WEST

Community has been important in the Christian world and notably in the church from its very beginnings. One can locate these beginnings in the community of the twelve apostles around Christ or in the still wider group of others sharing their life. The Christian experience seems to have begun in this way, and the notion of community becomes more specific in the Book of the Acts of the Apostles, which speaks of the believers having "all things in common" and meeting "for the breaking of bread in their homes,"[1] or, again, of "the multitude of believers" having "only one heart and one soul," and, once more, having "all things in common."[2] As a matter of fact, it is these quotations which were used as a basic text for the development of religious communities in the early church. Cassian quotes them to show the "apostolic origins" of the monastic life,[3] though his own experience of monastic life began in the desert. Augustine quotes them and makes them the very heart of his conception of community, with its notion of believers as being of "one heart and one mind."[4] So we have already, in these simple beginnings, some essential notes of Christian community, especially religious community. These are the ideas of the sharing of goods (and one must take these "goods" as including those of one's mind and heart,[5] of common (possibly liturgical) prayer, and of unity of minds and hearts—in other words, a tending toward a certain peace and love.

3

This paradisiacal picture is soon interrupted, even in the Book of Acts, by the story of the squabbles between Hellenistic and Jewish converts. Anyone who has lived in community will not be surprised. The ideal is high and beautiful; the reality is hard to achieve.

What were the roots of specifically monastic community—the first kind of religious community in the West as well as the East? When the conversion of Constantine made it safe—and "established"—to be a Christian, many who wanted to live their faith radically, as had the early martyrs, went out into the desert, notably in Egypt. In the Egyptian desert, people chose a spiritual father or mother to guide them in the ways of God, which were their ultimate goal. If several disciples lived with a given spiritual guide, this was a kind of community. These groups still considered their orientation to be eremitic or solitary, however, in contrast to the explicitly cenobitic, or monastic groups, for it was the "vertical" relation to God that was emphasized. The two ways are suggested by some of the desert anecdotes, or apophthegmata.

> A brother lived in the Cells and in his solitude he was troubled. He went to tell Abba Theodore of Pherme about it. The old man said to him, "Go, be more humble in your aspirations, place yourself under obedience and live with others." Later, he came back to the old man and said, "I do not find any peace with others." The old man said to him, "If you are not at peace either alone or with others, why have you become a monk? Is it not to suffer trials? Tell me how many years you have worn the habit?" He replied, "For eight years." Then the old man said to him, "I have worn the habit seventy years and on no day have I found peace. Do you expect to find peace in eight years?" At these words the brother went away strengthened.[6]

Here, living in community represents a "humbler aspiration" than living in solitude. This story suggests the desert scale of values as seen in many of its writings. But another story from the same source suggests the accent on realism in this regard.

> It was said of Abba John the Dwarf, that one day he said to his elder brother, "I should like to be free of all care, like the angels,

who do not work, but ceaselessly offer worship to God." So he took off his cloak and went away into the desert. After a week he came back to his brother. When he knocked on the door, he heard his brother say, before he opened it, "Who are you?" He said, "I am John, your brother." But he replied, "John has become an angel, and henceforth he is no longer among men." Then the other begged him saying, "It is I." However, his brother did not let him in, but left him there in distress until morning. Then, opening the door, he said to him, "You are a man and you must once again work in order to eat." Then John made a prostration before him, saying, "Forgive me."[7]

Another and different strand in the early tradition came from the communities of Pachomius. The latter saw his conversion as intimately connected with the common life since, when he asked God what he needed to do to do His will, the answer had to do with this common living. "The will of God is that you serve men in order to call them to him."[8] The term *koinonia* ("community") "is undoubtedly the key concept of Pachomian monasticism."[9] Life in the Pachomian monasteries was highly structured and centralized. This Pachomian tradition, however, has not continued into the present.

However, a tradition that has continued is that of Basil, in the East. His view of the hermit life was summarized in the now famous question, "If you are alone, whose feet will you wash?"[10] His "Rules" are a series of questions about Christian life and of answers drawn directly from Scripture. They have remained the inspiration of Orthodox religious life through the centuries.

In the West, as we have seen, Augustine was important. His original idea concerned priests living together, though tradition reports a community of nuns living the same Rule. Both his teaching and that of Basil, as well as the desert tradition through Cassian and earlier sources, influenced the strand of tradition that has continued through the centuries as the Benedictine Rule.

In one sense, there are probably as many theologies of monastic community, as lived in the Benedictine tradition, as there are monasteries. European communities often stress the idea of the monastic life as solitude with God. When a group of people wish to live the same ideal of solitude with God, they can help each other do this. Such a view accents the desert ideal. The Benedictine Rule stresses also the desire to live "under a Rule and an Abbot." In other words, obedience becomes an important ascetical theme, as does humility. But with these, solitude, charity, and peace remain from the earlier tradition. Benedict was also to add several new elements, some of which he drew from Augustine or Basil, and some from experience.

Stability was an innovation that Benedict stressed seriously. His chapter on the gyrovagues—monks who roamed from place to place—is a synopsis of the longer satire in the Rule of the Master. This latter gives one a good, if doubtless slanted, sketch of some of the experience of that time. Benedict's notion of the other kinds of monks—the sarabaites—is worth reflection as well. In his description:

> With no experience to guide them, no rule to try them . . . [they] have a character as soft as lead. Still loyal to the world by their actions, they clearly lie to God by their tonsure. Two or three together, or even alone, without a shepherd, they pen themselves up in their own sheepfolds, not the Lord's. Their law is what they like to do. . . . Anything they believe in and choose, they call holy; anything they dislike, they consider forbidden.[11]

Benedict's view of "true" monastic living can be inferred by contrast with the above. The selfishness and self-will that make any living together impossible are symbolized in "their own sheepfolds." The inability to be honest about motivations is seen as vitiating these people's choice. One is reminded of the hypocrisy with which Jesus charged the Pharisees and which is the danger of religious and moral people. Common living needs to build on truth.

Another new accent concerned manual work. The desert fathers and mothers did, indeed, work, but the notion of work as something serious and perhaps valuable in itself was not strong in the desert, as it had not been among the Greeks. For Benedict, it became part of the rhythm of the day in a new way, and manual work came into its own, also in new ways. Monks were not to be sad when they had to gather in the harvest themselves for "when they live by the labor of their hands then they are really monks."[12] Community living, then, had to do with this sharing as well.

Another new note was that of mutual obedience. In the desert one obeyed the spiritual guide. The presence of others was incidental. Not so for Benedict. If the abbot or abbess was to be obeyed first, nonetheless monks were to obey one another.[13] And the notions of mutual love, respect, and care are stressed.

> *They should each try to be the first to show respect to the other* (Rom. 12:10), supporting with the greatest patience one another's weaknesses of body or behavior, and earnestly competing in obedience to one another. No one is to pursue what he judges better for himself, but instead, what he judges better for someone else. To their fellow monks they show the pure love of brothers; to God, loving fear; to their abbot, unfeigned and humble love. Let them prefer nothing whatever to Christ. . . .[14]

Through the centuries in between, married people as well as monks have found inspiration in such lines as these. The ultimate, here, is love.

In the United States, Benedictine communities tend to stress community more than many of the European, at least in terms of their reflection on community. Cistercian communities also stress community, though in a very different way. Thomas Merton's struggles to find times and places of solitude reflect the notion of the common life as ascesis, practised in many Cistercian communities of both men and women, but his writing on the fruit of this ascesis also shows the purification of charity as its goal.[15] Once again, the struggle to find space as well as sharing seems to be a universal human experience.

These reflections have been historical and have dealt with the history of ideas. Before moving to more recent traditions of religious and lay life, let us try to see what happens today in the monastic communities that follow this older tradition.

A monastic community is normally a stable group of men or women choosing to live a common life under a common rule, or ideal, normally in the West that of Benedict. *Perfectae caritatis*, one of Vatican II's main statements on the religious life, has chosen to stress in this life-style that work is done basically within the confines of the monastery. This echoes the concern of Benedict's Rule that the monastery be self-sufficient so that the need for outings is minimized, though not wholly excluded. It is not necessary here to discuss to what extent other traditions, like the Carmelite or Franciscan, should be called monastic. If the Benedictine is taken as paradigmatic for the moment, necessary adjustments to reflect on the other traditions can easily be made.

In the Benedictine tradition, the community is *stable*—that is, it admits its own members and expects that, barring some extraordinary events, those members will be with it for life. Death, disease, and untoward events happen everywhere. Admissions, too, can radically change a community. Nonetheless, a certain stability of life in the group is a basic principle of this way of living. This element holds for most women's contemplative communities—for example, the Dominican, Franciscan (Poor Clare), and Carmelite—even where the corresponding masculine communities have chosen to classify themselves as "mendicants."

Another kind of stability comes from a certain kind of cloister, or separation from the world. Men and women, communities with and without apostolates, live these dimensions in very different ways. One finds everything from strict papal enclosure with almost no outside contacts to the large American or German abbeys with schools, seminaries, parishes, and other such activities. One can argue the degree to which some of these activities militate against the monastic ideal, but that is not the issue here. The typical monastic situation remains one in which the community lives together, prays together, gives priority to certain aspects of its life together and is basically against the centripetal aspects of some contemporary life-styles in communities. Writers of the last century and early in this often spoke of the familial model in this regard. The family in this case was the stable, centered Roman family with the *paterfamilias* at its head. Contemporary culture—notably American—has so radically changed from this model that new reflection on family models would be needed today. To understand the living of community and family today, however, it is important to understand how recent a phenomenon our present mobility is.

Finally, the monastic community lives a common ethos or spirit, summarized in Benedictine terms by the search for God. As was stated in the Introduction, people live together for help toward living this common project. Monastic solitude, silence, humility, obedience are all at the service of this central love which shows itself in mutual love, respect, and obedience. Benedict considered this life to be simply a living out of the Gospel, a life essentially "lay" and meant to be accessible. Perhaps this explains why so many who are not monks have used Benedict's Rule as an in spiration and guide through the ages. The monastery, then, was "a school of the Lord's service." This concept is important, though it must be remembered that a "school" at that time was not only a place to learn but a place where like-minded people gathered. The primary aim of this community is not, then, its work or ministry, nor is it cozy togetherness. The aim is learning together the ways of God, and one can see here a prototype of much community living in the centuries since.

What, then, are some of the elements of monastic community life as seen in the above picture? One could summarize them as including: a *common ideal or aim,* frequently that of solitude with God but certainly including a life of prayer and union with God; a *common authority* and notion of obedience, whether this involves the spiritual father or mother, as in the desert, or a more communitarian model, as in the Benedictine Rule (which still, however, leaves final judgment to the abbot); a *sharing of goods* (the Benedictine Rule would say, even to one's own body[16]); a *shared life of prayer,* notably liturgical; *stability* in the community with a related practice of enclosure of some sort; and a theology of *mutual peace, love, harmony,* and *obedience.* When, later, the vows of obedience, poverty, and chastity developed out of the earlier vows of *conversio morum,* stability, and obedience, one can see that all of this reflected an old tradition of trying to live out the love of God and others, the life of prayer and of Gospel teaching. Why did people choose to live this in community? If, originally a group gathered around a spiritual guide, later, it was the way a group of people lived its search for God and Gospel values that attracted others to join. A recent analysis by an American monk gives an excellent metaphor: if life is a dance, like the Jewish dance with the Torah, then those who come to a community like the dance movement they see there.[17]

This pattern, in a multitude of variations, held in the West for some thousand years, and it continues in the Christian East as well as in many monastic communities of non-Christian traditions. The variety is rich, even from house to house; the accents differ, but the basic thrust is much the same.

In the West the thirteenth century brought a surge of new currents in religious life. The church had become heavily institutionalized and wealthy. As one speaker was to say of the similar crisis before Vatican II, the bark of Peter was laden down with barnacles. A desire for a new, fresher approach, one more stripped down to essentials and, again, to the Gospel, made itself known. These currents led to the birth of what became known as the Mendicant Orders—the Franciscans and the Dominicans, who were later joined, for different reasons, by the Carmelites.

The female branches of these orders were to remain cloistered—not because of a difference of spirituality, basically, but because of sociological views on the nature of women's life and needs. But this fact eventually led to a difference of spirituality in the women's orders. (At present some of the women's communities of these traditions stress enclosure not only more strongly than their male counterparts but even more than the monastic order out of which their own growth came.)

The result of this bifurcation was that these cloistered women's communities lived the monastic spirituality already discussed, but with a different rule of life. The Poor Clares, cloistered Dominicans, and, later, the Carmelites, lived in smaller groups and under stricter discipline than the older monasteries, for they were born of an awareness of the need for reform and also out of a concern for poverty and for seriousness in Gospel living. The men's groups lived something different which was to begin a new current, moving into the present.

What was community like in these feminine groups? How did it differ from the earlier model? The same essential notes can be found there: a common spirituality directed basically toward union with God, a common authority, a sharing of goods, a shared life of prayer, stability in the community, and a certain accent on mutual love. Reaction to the recent past in the life of the church, however, led to a strictness of rule and life-style rather different from the past. Life in the desert or under Pachomius could be very austere indeed. But Christian monasticism was a new movement then with nothing in its own recent history against which to react. Abuses in monastic living had changed this scene. Poverty, austerity, and strictness became important in a new way. Where Benedict's Rule had been a balancing factor away from the excessive search for penance in the desert, the pendulum now swung the other way.

The swing was needed. If one reads the account of life in some medieval monasteries, one understands the surge of movements for reform. But it must also be said that if one reads some accounts of life in reformed monasteries, notably feminine, one can only wonder whether respect for the human had ceased to be a value at all. Women normally did not study theology or philosophy. Their lives were very much influenced by whatever group of men shared their basic ethos. But they applied this way of living within their own framework, constricted more and more by regulations of various sorts—notably rules about enclosure. Obedience, too, could be lived in a way which, while requiring great discipline and great renunciation, removed all sense of personal authority from those not entrusted with some office in the monastery. Some great women emerged from these various traditions and communities, and some great ideals and pieces of spiritual literature. But it is important to appreciate the constriction that characterized this stage of evolution of community living.

The male counterparts of these nuns were meanwhile facing a new challenge for their living of community. Monastic stability ceased to be an ideal for those called to a more itinerant lifestyle. Francis of Assisi spent some time in his hermitage and some on the roads, begging and preaching. Dominic was to call his community the Order of Preachers, and much of this preaching was on the roads as well. Even the Discalced Carmelites at the time of John of the Cross, though their roots were eremitical and their accent strongly on contemplation, moved from community to community as the calls of their religious life required. No longer did one enter a single community and stay there until death. It is not difficult to see what difference this single factor makes in the living of community.

If one joins a group of people to stay for the rest of one's life, it is clear to the one entering that, barring death or grave emergencies, he or she must work out the whole future with this given group. And the group, in accepting candidates, knows the same. In a community without this kind of stability, one can always hope that, if life is bad in this group, another group will be better. One can find more congenial as well as less congenial groups. There is always hope—and, in the days when communities were assigned rather than chosen, there was also fear. One might be blissfully happy but be moved tomorrow. For some this was an annual anxiety. For some, it still is. The effect on inner stability in this case is not difficult to see, though the ideal was that this kind of "hanging loose" promoted detachment.

While escape from present community tensions was a possible hope for the individual, moving difficult people around was also a possibility for superiors. Perhaps less care needed to be taken concerning admissions when this was the case. An itinerant life-style, too, removed some of the tensions and pressures in community. When there is work outside, some of the pressure of the same group of people always together in the same space is removed—or so it seems.

Community remained, however, of great importance in all these traditions: common liturgical prayer, a largely common horarium, a shared spirituality, and much that was still shared of the earlier monastic tradition, notably its basically contemplative thrust remained. Even the wish to be called "brother" in some of these traditions was significant.

The Counter-Reformation, however, brought with it still another thrust. Where the Mendicant Orders were clearly offshoots of the monastic tradition, new communities of priests who wanted to be religious but saw their first function in terms of their priesthood and apostolate came to the fore. Notable among these were the Jesuits. The description of Jesuit community as a barracks where one was always ready to go out to the battlefield occurs in more than one piece of literature.[18] The ascesis of many of these communities was equally strong and clear when compared to the earlier ideals: the demands were as great and the insistence on a contemplative vision was often strong. But this was an ascesis for soldiers of God, for workers in the fields of the Lord, rather than for a family or community living together its common consecration from which any apostolic work flowed. Strong characters and saintly ones emerged from such training. One thinks of Francis Xavier, Ignatius of Loyola, and saints of other communities with similar thrusts. But in many ways the Jesuits remain the prototype of this kind of spirituality, partly because their influence on other orders has been so strong. The Spiritual Exercises alone have been formative for many other orders of religious of both sexes.

In this context, what happens to the common elements of community mentioned earlier? A common ideal or aim remains,

but the first priority is no longer a common search for God—
expressed, frequently, by a common liturgical life and office.
Much of the common aim is concerned with apostolic ministry,
though this draws its life from prayer.

A common authority and obedience remain and must even,
in some cases, be stronger, for the people thus unified are spread
further abroad. A sharing of goods remains important, but it
must often take different forms. Stability in community is, of
course, excluded. Mutual peace, love, and harmony may be
stressed but the accent is more toward the outside, the apostolate.
Community life, now, has become something very different.

This development was to grow in new ways with the centuries
after the Renaissance. Bit by bit women's communities began to
emerge, born more often of an awareness of one or another need
of the people around them rather than arising from an inner
call to consecration or prayer. The Visitandines wanted, as their
name indicates, to visit those in need but the requirement of enclosure for women soon turned them into a community living a
classical contemplative life. The Ursulines—paradigmatic of what
would happen to many others—began as what we would now
call a secular institute, a group of women living for God in their
homes. In Angela Merici's original vision, "They were to labour
for the salvation of the world through the upbringing and training of children and girls."[19] But "every bishop who founded a
group of Ursulines modified the Brescian rule according to his
own ideas."[20] Soon there were "simultaneously secular Ursulines,
Ursulines gathered in community without vows or enclosure, and
Ursuline Monials."[21] Under Charles Borromeo, "secular Ursulines and those in community formed one and the same Company
of St. Ursula with two ways of life"[22] and the communities of
"monials" were, like other monastic communities, to become basically autonomous and independent, though united in congregations. What is interesting, though, is that the recruitment of
monials was to be from among the elite of the Company:

> The distinction is clear: community life was judged to be of a
> higher order than the life led by the majority of the Company,
> and only the elite were to be received. Community life became an
> end in itself, sought for its ascetical value and not for an apostol-
> ic end.[23]

This pattern of movement was to characterize more than one community of women begun for apostolic reasons.

Again and again, as the years progressed, groups of women began doing social work, teaching the young, nursing, cate-chizing—often but not always at the request of some local eccle-siastic or male religious—and soon they would become a group of religious with more or less ecclesiastical approval. But becom-ing religious had its drawbacks for the apostolate. Vincent de Paul's Daughters of Charity finally opted not to become legally religious if that status would too severely limit their ability to serve the poor. Other religious women went through this struggle in various ways and with varying results. Some felt their apos-tolates were a first priority and even began by saying they did not want to become religious if the laws that resulted would ham-per them too seriously. Others wanted to be religious first but also wanted to serve and had to try to juggle these two require-ments of their vocations within ecclesiastical regulations not re-quired of men.

What was the effect of all this on the living of religious com-munity among such women? First of all, the accent, in many cases, moved "outward"—toward work, rather than toward mutual help in living an ethos. But, in fact, forming a community at all was still about sharing. So an intrinsic tension came to be built in— one familiar to many "nonreligious." Another effect was certainly the consciousness of the need to "toe the line" with regard to regulations. Almost all foundresses had been given lists of re-quirements sometimes a little foreign and sometimes very foreign to their original aims and desires. Some founded communities which they wanted very prayer-centered in thrust but open to various forms of the apostolate, and these found obligations like enclosure and office in choir less burdensome. Others really wanted to be out working for the poor and needy and felt them-selves held back at every step, at least if they wished to be "really religious" and apostolic, too. All, however, if they wished eccle-siastical approval as religious, had to obey and were visited to see that they did. The accent on regulations grew stronger and stronger in the years leading toward Vatican II—an accent mov-ing away from the earlier one on a spirituality or the rule of life which expressed it, or even on the unifying force of an apostolate. If national characteristics have something to do with this, the large numbers of communities founded in France and the large numbers of Irish religious as well, meant, in some cases, that Jansenist tendencies were combined with the already heavy stress on regulations.

It is of the utmost importance to note the distinction between rules and Rules. A community living together because it is gathered around a common spirituality expressed by a document called a Rule—often an ancient Rule born of a still older tradition—has, paradoxically, a relativizing element at its very heart. This document expresses a spirituality, and an old one, which needs to be adapted to different times. It is itself a fruit of an older, and probably adapted, tradition and needs to be seen in that light. There are numerous strands in the inheritance by which such a community lives—*if* the level of spiritual education in the house is such that candidates are trained in the sources of the community's spiritual heritage. This kind of rule is the instrument for the transmission of a living tradition belonging to the charism of a given community.

The other kind of rule is a regulation imposed by some authority for a certain uniformity of behavior. When imposed by ecclesiastical authority on certain groups of people who come out of different traditions, such rules can produce a certain, possibly very healthy, common activity. Roman Catholics through the ages celebrate the periods of preparation for Christmas and Easter in certain ways because of a certain disciplinary and ascetic tradition that has long been incarnated in certain rules. This has been a common experience in very different countries and cultures and has often also been a bond and a help.

When rules begin to be multiplied, however—when they become detailed and, at times, inappropriate to the living situation of those to whom they apply—difficulties occur. In the case of religious women from recently founded congregations, rules were often taken out of monastic sources and applied to situations where they did not fit. Worst of all, they were taught to those in formation in a way divorced from the source from which the rules were born. One thinks, for example, of the Benedictine great silence, from the time of the last office at night until after the office in the morning. When one reflects that Benedict suggests that one can gently encourage those who are too sleepy to want to get themselves to the earliest office in the morning, one can only conclude that his view of this night silence was that it was extremely important but was to be intelligently applied.[24] In the years before Vatican II, however, there were stories of religious, who, when their house was on fire at night, let others know this by sign so as not to break the night silence! Such stories are told of monasteries as well. They are indicative of a situation that made the changes of Vatican II necessary for all Christians, not just religious. It is not only religious who suffer from the effects of legalism and moralism.

It seems safe to say, in view of the literature—and the memories common to many religious who lived before the council—that however strong the emphasis on the other elements of community life the stress on regulations often laid a heavy burden on communities. The accent was taken off the common authority, and even off the spirit and Rule, and placed on these regulations of which the superior became the enforcer. Rare and fortunate were the communities where the latter was in the first instance a spiritual guide and inspiration. Suffering from the authority of superiors was considered to be normal. Normal it is, from the earliest ages of the desert. But it is one thing to suffer because one is seeking God and union, and because obedience is imposed to help in following Christ, and quite another thing to suffer because the superior has become an enforcer of regulations. Obviously, fine lines can never be drawn here. But the accent certainly changed. If one wanted to exaggerate the importance of this stress on rules, one could say that in preconciliar years: (1) the common ideal had, for many communities, become the perfect living of all these small rules; (2) the common authority had become an enforcer of these rules, as well as the person who decided and controlled one's work; (3) the sharing of goods was worked out in terms of a series of regulations "on the practice of poverty," which freed one from much reflection on the meaning of poverty and why one would choose it; (4) the shared life of prayer was, for many communities, weighed down with obligations for vocal prayers and cursorily said offices without much accent on what was helpful for deeper prayer and union with God; (5) stability no longer held, except insofar as one made no personal choices but was sent "wherever obedience called"; (6) mutual peace, love, and harmony were still stressed but, in a tenser life-style than before, they were often achieved by the repression of contrary feelings.

It is clear that the living of community had become a very different thing from what was originally sought and lived. Even if the above picture overemphasizes the blacker side of things— even if many religious had a truly happy experience of community before the council, as, indeed, very many did—nonetheless, it is clear that what began as a natural growth ceased to be held together by organic development. Much came to be enforced from without. It was inevitable that the dam would break.

Vatican II changed many things in the living of community. One of the most essential of the changes was the movement from large institutional communities to small ones where personal relationships were more possible. In monastic settings, different means were taken to achieve this same possibility for more realistic relating.

Another major change was in the attitude of such authority figures as remained. Many apostolic communities, notably feminine and American, dispensed with superiors. Many monastic groups stressed collegiality and consensus. Superiors became servants of the house, listeners, enablers—at least, such was the ideal.

With regard to poverty, prayer, and mutual love, accents went off rules and onto realism. What would actually help this particular religious to pray, love, and be poor? Of course, there were—and are—abuses. One could make a case that religious today are no longer poor, obedient, prayerful, ascetic, and many other things. While it is true that what religious "say" and witness to by their lives is more important than their words, it is equally true that doing something just to "witness" smacks of acting. Where religious community today really seeks the values of the Gospel, the witness will be present. Where it does not, it is surely best for everyone to see this clearly.

An essential point of the council's work was the invitation to return to sources—the Gospel and the charism of founders.[25] Other values stressed were a healthy adaptation to contemporary culture and life as well as participation in the life of the church. Cloister was no longer required or encouraged for apostolic communities—a fact which led to radical changes of mentality and life-style, as will be seen below. This change also allowed community living to be more "open" to visitors or even to participants who were not themselves religious. The development of Protestant communities like Taizé also affected the spirituality of community life in these years.

Our question, for present purposes, then, is this. What—in this church of the late twentieth century—is religious community today? If one forgets the past and just looks at present phenomena, what does one see? Doubtless, apostolic and contemplative groups should be looked at separately, with monasticism seen as a group different from both because resistant to categories.

It seems safe to say (as a working hypothesis to be confirmed by some of the cases on which we will reflect) that most communities of apostolic religious today are small groups, often without a local superior, where members work in different capacities and often in different places. The meeting time is usually the evening meal and perhaps prayer after the day's work. What regulations exist are often born of the group itself—or some personalities in it! (This does not deny that there are groups still living in large houses or institutions, that not a few have local superiors, and so on. Our cases will reflect on some of this.)

Where do these apostolic groups stand with regard to the elements of earlier community seen above? While they are usually members of the same congregation or order, their reasons for coming together in a particular house are often likely to be based on the needs of a given apostolate rather than on common in-depth reflection on life-style or choices. The fact that they belong to the same order may lead them to believe they have much in common along these lines but the individuals may differ radically in their concrete ways of living their "charism." Ways of living a single community's charism differ more from person to person now than they have for many decades, if not centuries. Some apostolic religious would say that their spirituality today is meant to be centered in their ministry or apostolate and therefore that community is very secondary. This view will be recognized as similar to the early Jesuit one. Later chapters in this book will discuss this option—helpful for some individuals, damaging for others. And still other active religious will say that their main community is found outside the house. So individual small communities are often characterized less by a particular way of living a particular charism than simply by the people in them and the way they live, for their choice of each other was often made in light of convenience for ministry or closeness to work. Such communities are more open to others than in the past and freer for the varied apostolic works of their members than before. By these same gifts, however, they also run the risk of becoming very dispersed.

In these communities, there is often no common authority—at least locally—though there is one for larger decisions on another geographic level. The sharing of goods is practiced in different ways by almost each different group. While people outside religious community often comment that it no longer seems that all things are held in common or that the life-style is poor, there are in fact forms of sharing in almost every house. (The case of religious living alone is not dealt with here, though it will be below.)

Most communities have some form of shared prayer, though one can safely say that there is a widespread questioning of these forms. In some circles, the questioning has led to at least a temporary choice not to pray together. Individual religious may pray much, but sharing of prayer seems more difficult. Stability, of course, is not an element of this life-style. In many communities the people within them change each year, and the option to change is one that some religious look at annually. The implications of this constant change for lasting relationships and the ability or inability to share options is a question I find insufficiently discussed in many of these circles. Finally, the questions around mutual peace, love, and harmony have come to the fore in a new way. Simple politeness is no longer seen as sufficient for real relationship. Repression of conflict—internally or externally—is less and less valued, though fatigue and need for relative peace may make this a pragmatic requirement, and the old training still makes honesty about feelings and assertiveness difficult for some. The aim of setting up small communities was, in the thought of many, to facilitate real relating. It remains to be seen whether this aim will be achieved.

Finally, another important change is the greater respect for individual liberty, differences, and charisms—though this is found in many monastic settings as well. People are really given space, in many cases, to grow and become themselves. This makes for richer community living—and more open differences as well. But it is an element of great health—for each one and for the whole.

One important element in this whole question is that of silence. In the past, many communities had rules of silence of varying degrees of strictness. This safeguarded time, a certain degree of solitude, a certain privacy and space. It also prevented some challenge, wear and tear, and honesty. At present, few active communities keep silence. Each person has to protect his or her own time, solitude, and space, and this can sometimes be very difficult. In some cases people go for years without realizing the cause of some of their tension and strain. The climate of different communities varies greatly, from those in which there is always speaking, television, or music to those where basically there is much quiet. The size and location of houses has much to do with this. A conclusion to be drawn from all this reflection is that the small apostolic community today is a very different phenomenon from very many of the religious communities of the past. One could even wonder whether it is not fundamentally different from the beginnings of its own particular congregation. Where the older communities were together in order to live a certain kind of life with certain definite characteristics and often a largely contemplative aim, present small communities, while sharing the basic spirituality of their order, are often together for largely pragmatic reasons. And often that same spirituality, for historical reasons, furthers this pragmatic stance, as when it is said that the reason for coming together is to fulfill a certain work. Reflection on community has been thought by some to be navel gazing, and one understands this impatience in the sense that people coming together to marry come for each other and not for the marriage. Nonetheless, if community in itself is not seen as having value apart from supplying bed and breakfast and a certain companionship to back one's work, then we are truly into a totally different phenomenon from the religious community of the past.

A question that needs serious reflection is that of evolution. As was said, apostolic communities were often founded for a work. Then they evolved, became religious congregations, with community life, religious life. Sometimes a more contemplative style became important in the process of evolution. All of this becomes part of the charism and cannot just be swept away[26] or ignored. But at present it is still difficult to know how to integrate all this theologically.

Alongside the apostolic communities, change has also occurred among contemplatives. In many cases, what has happened is an adaptation of life-style in the direction of more respect for the human, more reflection on the values older rules were trying to attain; a suppler and more evangelical understanding of authority and obedience; a relativization of austerity when compared to other values like charity. In many cases, there has been serious reflection on the original charism with a readiness to let go of more recent and not useful accretions.

These changes are positive, but there have been negatives as well. As among other religious, there are disagreements about what to keep and what to give up. Contemplatives, as well as active religious, have been known to throw out the baby with the bathwater—or, on the other hand, to refuse to change in any appreciable way for want of ability to distinguish essentials from accidentals. Among contemplative women there has been the struggle to know how much human development is helpful to the furtherance of the contemplative charism and how much defeats that purpose. They have to steer between the Scylla of giving up all that is specific in their lives and the Charybdis of denying the human basis in which the whole mystery of union takes place. (Why, however, has this been easier for many men's groups? Or has it?)

In the case of monastics, active/contemplative distinctions are foreign to a life-style older than such distinctions and seen as embracing what God sends and the community discerns as appropriate. Monastic communities have, in many cases, changed radically—often as radically as the apostolic. But the changes have been different. Some communities have managed to work through a common search to find the essentials of the monastic vocation and to judge all observances in terms of that end. This is the ideal. As in all things human, communities struggle between giving up so much of the observance that helps to the end are also lost and, on the other hand, refusing the necessary challenge. In many ways, their life-style is less changed than that of the active communities. Where the importance of the office remains, this gives a certain character to the day and to prayer. Where the essential elements of the horarium have been rethought and rechosen, the fundamental values are still those of early Monte Cassino, for example, though clothed in different forms. The computer may have replaced the copying of manuscripts; theology classes may have replaced the memorizing of the Psalms; but the basic orientation of the life with its rootedness in the Word of God and the world of nature is often very akin to the past. What has doubtless changed most is the concept of the *fuga mundi*, the "flight from the world." Benedict and Anthony may have fled a decaying Roman Empire; monks today are often more concerned with their world. Thomas Merton writing on racism and the Vietnam War may be less an exception than one would think, even for communities with a very strict orientation. Raimundo Panikkar and Myriam Dardenne speak of an integration no longer by exclusion but by inclusion.[27] So here there seems more continuity than rupture.

Where has this long exploration taken us? In cursory form it has sketched some of the development of religious community in the West through the centuries. We will look at other types of communities—those of marriage and family, for example. After some reflection on case material, it may be possible to draw conclusions on community living in a wider sense, with religious community as a springboard for the beginning of this reflection. This chapter's examination was largely based on history. Another, based on psychology, seems appropriate now.

·2·

COMMUNITY—DEAD OR ALIVE?

Readers acquainted with Jungian literature will recognize in the title of this chapter a reference to a work by Adolf Guggenbühl-Craig, *Marriage—Dead or Alive*.[1] The thesis of this work is that we in the West have a tendency to see marriage as a source of well-being or happiness. One thinks of films ending with a couple walking hand in hand into the sunset, of fairy tales concluding with the marriage of the prince and princess, after which "they lived happily ever after." But this, according to Guggenbühl, is not truly what marriage is about—nor is it a state of life into which people should enter indiscriminately just to legitimize sexual activity, to have children, or to enjoy security and status. One has to be called to live a true marriage, he believes, and what such a marriage is about is not well-being, comfort, security, or happiness, but rather individuation, even salvation in the psychological sense of that word.

What is individuation in the thought of this author? Following Jung, he sees individuation as an essential drive of the human psyche. "Individuation is as essential a part of human motivation as hunger, thirst, aggression, sexuality, and pressures toward finding relaxation and attaining happiness."[2] The human soul experiences the need to develop, to "differentiate itself . . . and develop itself individually."[3] It needs to become more conscious and to integrate more of the unconscious aspects of its personality. Guggenbühl stresses that this process need not take place only in analysis, for the whole point of his book is the possible use of marriage as a help toward individuation. Finally, "the drive

23

to individuation impels us to make contact with an inner spark of divinity, which Jung described as the self."[4] It is important to remember that for many Jungians, the word *self* in such a context is usually capitalized, for it refers to something deeper, greater, wider, and more personal than the individual self of the person involved.

The basic idea of Guggenbühl's book can be as applicable to questions of religious community life as to marriage. True, in religious community one does not find two people vowing to live together forever, but one does find people permanently vowed to a common commitment living together very closely—and even too closely for some temperaments. Another common factor between marriage and religious life is the fact that this life-style precludes making one's own decisions as one likes without being forced always to take into consideration the other or others with whom one lives. It has become increasingly common to distinguish the vocation or call to religious life, notably apostolic, from the call involved in the life of secular institutes by the primary factor of call to live in community.[5] (This issue will be more fully discussed below, especially with regard to the evolution of individuals within a religious community. For the present let us keep in mind this parallel between the vocation to community and Guggenbühl's notion of the call to what he terms "individuation marriage.")

To develop his concept of individuation further, Guggenbühl draws on different fairy tales, myths, and art works that depict the journey toward individuation as a struggle with the obstacles arising along the way. St. George kills the dragon; the fairy-tale prince conquers obstacles to marry the princess; in a Welsh legend, the hero Culhrwch struggles through many violent and dangerous adventures to win his bride, symbol of his soul:

> Courage, cowardice, chaotic fighting, filth, and the gruesome imbibing of witches' blood characterize this story. In contrast, elegant detachment and distance are portrayed in the pictures of St. George and the dragon.
>
> Individuation is better depicted and symbolized in the bloody and chaotic story of Culhrwch than in the image of the elegant knight St. George.
>
> Individuation means an active, difficult, uncomfortable working

through of one's own complex psyche towards a joining of its opposites; these opposites are symbolized by man and woman.[6]

The process of individuation, then, is neither easy nor painless. Guggenbühl sees the journey as necessarily bloody, one way or another, if we are to attain the end our spirit seeks. In other views, the path to individuation can be calmer and simpler than this, but it is always the *individual's* journey. Marriage, then—and, for the religious, the struggles of life with both God and community—supplies the raw materials and the "obstacles to conquer" for this growth process.

One of the main issues to be dealt with in man-woman relations on the way to individuation is that of a man's relation to his mother—nourishing, devouring, spiritual, or whatever else she may have been—and a woman's parallel relation to her father. Only after these primary battles have been fought can the issues simply of the feminine or masculine be approached.

> It requires great psychological effort for a man to reach the point of understanding that these archetypal powers of the psyche inhere in himself, and that it avails nothing to see them only in his natural mother or to project them onto other women or onto institutions; to reach to the point of seeing that nothing is accomplished by railing against his mother or by leveling repeated accusations against society.[7]

It is not difficult to see the applicability of this observation to the living of religious or other community. We all come into community life, as into marriage, carrying images from the past still insufficiently integrated. Learning not to project these onto others is a long process. Authority figures are the easiest target, but so is any other person who is powerful, gifted, a leader, manipulative, or simply very different from us. It is a long struggle to the discovery that most of the passions aroused by these issues have to do with my own inner world and conflicts, rather than with the ordinary—or even less ordinary—flesh-and-blood people around me. Few people or institutions have the authority and power our complexes tend to project onto them. When one can finally stop placing the blame for things outside, whether on people or on society, a first step toward maturation has been taken.

The next step is, as Guggenbühl says, the coming to terms with the *contrasexual,* the masculine for a woman, the feminine for a man. It is easy to see why marriage would be an ideal—if not easy!—situation for the working out of this part of one's development. But what happens to religious living in same-sex communities, notably those with few contacts outside their own group?

It has been said that the more restricted the contacts with the opposite sex, the more the contrasexual element emerges in images or dreams—or perhaps in the intensity with which one experiences the encounters one does have. Or perhaps it is simply some temperaments rather than others for whom this particular struggle is paramount. One thinks of the "temptations" of the desert fathers as seen in Hieronymus Bosch's picture of St. Anthony. Not just wild beasts but beautiful women were often the content of the inner world of imagery for such men. Is this abnormal and to be sneered at as the sign that their life was unhealthy, or is it, on the contrary, very normal and healthy? The relation with the contrasexual must be dealt with and integrated, whether this be through external contacts or through those in the psyche. The only danger would be the effort to repress the inner or to escape the outer—and the full emotional effects of the outer—to which one is called.

The purpose of this process is the growth in ability not only to develop in oneself the necessary qualities of the opposite sex— call them strength and tenderness, to oversimplify[8]—but also to develop the relational abilities that result, the power to deal with others out of a centered and integrated psyche, without fear of being truly oneself. Both the inner struggles and the outer are part of this process and they both further progress toward the goal. The specific issue of same-sex communities is also that of each individual. As a totally "masculine" man with no feminine characteristics is ultimately only half a person, so is such a community. And the same principle holds for women. The aim is not the production of feminine men and masculine women— though one does meet such—but rather the development of harmonized personalities able to interact relationally in a mature way. In community, as in marriage, the path to this end is through struggle and not through escape, tempting though such an escape may sometimes be.

Guggenbühl speaks also of the necessity of dealing with evil, suffering, death, "the destructive side of God, of the world, and of our own soul."[9] This facing of the inner and outer shadow is a sine qua non for the individuation process: in both marriage and community situations, looking squarely at these elements, particularly those that cannot change, and learning to live with them realistically is an essential part of the process of individuation. Guggenbühl speaks of the illusion inherent in a concept of salvation to which I might wish to make others submit. Bloody wars have been fought in the name of reform, and the same is true of communities. But salvation is a personal task and I only further another's "work" to the degree to which I do my own. I cannot interfere in the individual struggle between that other and his or her God.

Does it follow that the search for individuation is a wholly self-centered process? No, since whatever I am not willing to struggle through in my own personal life, I can in no way expect other people or institutions to do. If I cannot stop projecting and work my way through to some kind of peace, it is hardly surprising when, on a national level, the enemy is still always out there somewhere and evil, rather than being within our gates where the first solutions need to take place. Further, the individuated person, however solitary his or her life, relates in a deep way to the whole of the cosmos. In Jungian terms, contact with the collective unconscious and the Self involves contact with everything else. In the Christian tradition, the solitary was seen from the beginning as "separated from all but united to all."[10]

Before reflecting in more detail on the implications of Guggenbühl's thought for community living, let us look at a few more of the ideas in his book. An early chapter speaks of the apparently negative sides of marriage—its ability to thwart and frustrate a couple—as well as the reaction of many therapists to such a situation.

> A psychoanalysis has two goals: to free the patient from his neurotic suffering, and further, to help him toward his own full development and toward finding the meaning of his life. Very often, however, psychoanalysis ends a marriage with a divorce. To find meaning in life means, in this case, first of all determining that the marriage does not allow any sort of meaningful development for the analysand.[11]

He spells out what this last sentence might mean:

> Two people of different sex, usually with extremely different im-
> ages, fantasies, and myths, with differing strength and vitality,
> promise one another to be with each other night and day, so to
> speak, for a whole lifetime. Neither of them is supposed to spoil
> the other's experience, neither is supposed to control the other,
> both of them should develop all their potentials fully. This mighty
> oath is often declared, however, only because of an overwhelming
> sexual intoxication.[12]

Religious, particularly older ones, would take exception to some
of the above points, notably as applied to the religious life. (Our
grandmothers might have as well.) While they would (usually)
agree on the importance of healing neurotic suffering, many tend
to believe that full development or self-fulfillment are selfish
goals, that the meaning of life is better found through some
measure of sacrifice. We shall see that, to a considerable degree,
Guggenbühl would agree. On the other hand, if a marriage (or
a community situation) truly "does not allow any sort of meaningful development" for the person in question, then it really
does seem that some questions need to be asked. We have only
one lifetime and its purpose cannot be to stifle all potential for
development—especially because of a choice made in early youth,
be it "because of an overwhelming sexual intoxication" or because
of an equally deep religious desire or dream.

Most of us know people who have gone into therapy with the
result that they have abandoned their marriage or their religious
life. Guggenbühl refers to this phenomenon again and again.
Partly it has to do with some presuppositions of the therapist,
he will say.[13] But partly, also, the issue can be the kind of experience of stifling mentioned above. Numbers of religious would
not agree that others in community must agree not to spoil their
experience, never to control them, never to impede their full
development of all potentials. People are slightly more realistic
than this in a community situation. Indeed, some religious may
well go in the other direction and believe it normal that their
experience be spoiled, that they be controlled and their development impeded. They may say all of this is part of their sacrifice.
The difficulty is, of course, that where minimal space, development, and liberty are not present the same thing happens

spiritually and psychologically as happens physically. One becomes cramped, even warped; necessary powers atrophy. One can become totally out of touch with personal authority and power; very lacking in freedom; and, finally, all the things one has pushed out of consciousness as one renounced them can come back to haunt one in other ways. Psychosomatic illness, odd little idiosyncracies, attachment to trifles, loss of a sense of proportion—these and so many other symptoms reflect this loss of personal autonomy and space. And everyone who has lived in community (including many family members) knows the person who is all self-sacrifice and yet who gives unceasing nonverbal messages as to what others must and must not do and as to what his or her own needs and requirements are—to which everyone else must conform. And there are others who simply give the impression of having been beaten.

For younger religious who have entered well after Vatican II, the ideal described by Guggenbühl may seem more real. They may be astonished to be asked for sacrifice, to have their space invaded and their freedom limited, depending on the kind of formation they have received. And what is partly true for them may be even more true of some of the middle-aged who have now asserted their independence. Each individual is at a different stage in a personal evolution that is part of an ecclesial and social evolution as well.

For we must never forget that our grandfathers and grandmothers and the generations before them took much of the sacrifice mentioned above as much for granted as did their religious peers. In recent decades—partly due to recent psychologies—some of these views have changed.

Be all this as it may, the point at present is that marriages—as well as religious lives—can be entered into with false expectations and that both marriage and the religious life can come to seem truly what Guggenbühl calls an instrument of torture set up by society and from which some therapists wish to free their clients. On this point he remarks, "marriage and family structure are something 'unnatural,' not instinctive, an artificial product of human effort."[14] "This is why we find so many different forms of marriage in the course of history and among various cultures."[15] The same is true of methods for child rearing. It is we and our culture who set up the ideals for marriage and the family, and these are a specifically human and not just "natural" choice.

It is here that Guggenbühl sets up the distinction between well-being and salvation.

> Well-being has to do with the avoidance of unpleasant tensions, with striving for the possession of a physical sense of comfort, relaxed and pleasant. The state of well-being requires having sufficient nourishment, protection from the elements, an absence of anxiety about one's continuing existence, an easing of sexual tension now and then, and a pleasant though not exhausting amount of physical activity.[16]

He adds that a minimum of space for living is needed, and he relates this notion of well-being to that of happiness. Salvation, however, is related to the search for God, with the struggles and seeking for meaning that this latter imposes. The two paths are not mutually exclusive nor totally separate, but they are certainly not identical.

The question then arises: where, in this view, does marriage fit? Is it meant to supply well-being—that is, comfort, relaxation, a pleasant life, protection? Or is it meant to be a path to salvation, to individuation? We have already seen that our author's position is the latter. Marriage is usually celebrated with a religious ceremony, he recalls, but religion is not the only reason.

> One of the essential features of this soteriological pathway is the absence of avenues for escape. Just as the saintly hermits cannot evade themselves, so the married persons cannot avoid their partners. In this partially uplifting, partially tormenting evasionlessness lies the specific character of this path.[17]

Anyone who has lived in community will be able to resonate to this point. Even in communities which are not "stable" for life, one can no more escape the others than a husband can his wife. One can go out, where there is no enclosure. One can be "busy," too occupied to share in the common life, and how frequent this is! One can be ill or whatever other evasion one can manage. But still, the root of life is there, in the house where one lives—together. And I believe that many religious who use the above evasions know it. Remarks about "bed and breakfast" communities are too frequent not to suggest this.

Once again, remarks Guggenbühl, love is as important in the Christian concept of salvation as it is in marriage.

> Marriage is one of the soteriological pathways of love, but of a love that is not altogether identical with what is produced by the wanton youth Cupid. Cupid's love is not to be counted on, is moody, unrestricted. The peculiarity of the love that marks the soteriological pathway of marriage is its "anti-natural" stability: "For better or for worse, for richer or for poorer, in sickness and in health, until death do us part.". . . The love on which marriage rests transcends the "personal relationship" and is more than merely relational.[18]

Marriage is not the pathway to salvation for everyone, he concludes. It is a vocation. "The goal would be to reserve marriage only for those people who are especially gifted in finding their salvation in the intensive, *continuous* relationship and dialectical encounter between man and woman."[19]

This last statement has profound significance for those called to live community life. If this continuous encounter and dialectic is seen as a burden, a harsh necessity, something to avoid, is the call to community really there? That such an experience can be harsh and demanding has been the constant theme of the spirituality of religious life through the centuries. John of the Cross will speak of community as an experience—painful—of mutual polishing[20]; Benedict will say that it is in the militia of the common life that one learns the discipline needed for the solitary struggle in the desert.[21] But in both cases, the implication is that one truly lives in community, with all the pain this can afford, knowing the positive it affords as well. If one wants simply to live in community side by side, avoiding real relationship, honesty, and "rocking the boat," can the question as to any real call to community not be asked here as well? I do not believe—nor, I think, does Guggenbühl believe about marriage—that community is so horizontal a relationship as to overshadow the vertical. In fact, I would tend strongly in the opposite direction. But I also do not believe that a relating to God in truth permits a relation to others that is unreal, superficial, or false. One need not spend hours upon hours interacting or at meetings, but what relationships and contacts there are need to be true. And, on occasion, hours may be needed to build or heal this truth.

Guggenbühl's next observations elaborate on this point. "Masculine and feminine do not harmonize."[22] He begins by pointing out the fallacy of believing that there is only one feminine or masculine archetype. There are many ways to be either, symbolized throughout mythology and art and history. We need to be in touch with those of our day. Furthermore, one passes from one archetype to another as one moves through the various stages of life.

> For a further understanding of marriage it is very important to realize not only that masculine and feminine can relate to one another through hostility, but that they don't even have to be "relating" at all. There are many archetypally feminine ways of relating in which a man plays no part whatsoever, and many archetypally masculine ways which have no connection to the feminine. Man and woman, therefore, complement one another only partially. Marriage can be really understood properly only when we free ourselves from the "harmony complex."[23]

Men and women can "jostle" each other, he adds; they can draw together as much in annihilation and rejection as in love. "A marriage may well be built around existential solitariness, which had not been recognized for what it was"[24]—a point worth serious reflection in communities where a certain growth in solitariness may be a normal fruit of precisely the life that has been chosen, with its orientation to God and, frequently, growth in prayer. He adds that all these factors of "unharmony" need not always have to do with neurosis or neurotic relationship.

> Marriage is not comfortable and harmonious; rather, it is a place of individuation where a person rubs up against himself and against his partner, bumps up against him in love and in rejection, and in this fashion learns to know himself, the world, good and evil, the heights and the depths.[25]

Some of these ideas are obviously more applicable to marriage than to relationships that are less permanent or involve more people. Nonetheless, it has lessons for a community situation. If the people involved are true to themselves and honest with each other (though, even when they are not, some of these things occur), there will be rubs and bumps, love and rejection. And the result will be growth in self-knowledge and knowledge of the world, of others, of God. The price for the attainment of this result is the readiness to live out the community situation in truth, not seeking to palliate all differences and take the easiest way to solve every problem. It is the reality quotient in all of this that is salvific.

Guggenbühl speaks at length of sexuality. The points he makes will be considered in a later chapter on the relationships between sexuality and solitude in community. One point, however, is important here. After speaking of the dangers of a concept of "normal" sexuality that would severely restrict both partners not only in their sexual expression but even in their ability to allow themselves to face and share their real fantasies, he remarks:

> It never happens, therefore, that in marriage two completely "healthy" people get together. . . . But marriage does not have to do with one partner's curing the other, or even with one's changing the other significantly; this is not possible. Through the act of getting married, one has taken on the task of mutual confrontation until death. . . . The neurotic symptoms too will have to be synchronized with one another. The peculiarities of oneself and of one's partner must be borne, accepted, and integrated into the interplay between the spouses. . . . In the individuation marriage, both partners confront each another with everything, with the healthy and the sick, the normal and the abnormal traits of their essential being.[26]

The notion of "confrontation until death" may arouse horror. I do not believe, however, that Guggenbühl uses this term in the sense of popular psychology. He is speaking, rather, of two people facing each other with the whole of their beings, just as they are—with their sickness, their neuroses, their health, and all the rest. And they can do that only if it is safe to share the neuroses. Relationships in communities are clearly not as intimate as marriage. Nonetheless, if people are truly themselves rather than presenting fronts of appropriate behavior to each other; if they say what they truly feel, think, and experience, rather than saying the expected or appeasing—then something of the salvific dynamic that Guggenbühl mentions can occur. People will not change, as he says; nor are we together to change them. But remaining who we are, we can learn to live out together the mutual "dance" of this common life.

> Many marriages dry up and miss the path to individuation because the couples try to ease their situations through excluding and repressing their most important essential characteristics, whether these be peculiar sexual wishes, neurotic traits, or whatever. The more one confronts everything, the more interesting and fruitful becomes the path to individuation.[27]

It goes without saying that the same holds true in communities, even if the level of intimacy is normally lower.

It becomes important, here, to raise the question of time and psychic energy. In apostolic groups especially, people return home after a hard day, and they want peace and quiet and not "confrontation." They may not even want interest. They may just want peace. In contemplative groups, a day structured around prayer, office, and work can be much more time-filling than outsiders know. Where is the time to be found for such interaction as the above—and is it even desirable in a life oriented toward contemplation and union with God?

These two questions are different. In the first, it would seem that the essential question for each individual and for the group is that of expenditure of psychic energy and time. Do people really want the lion's share of both to go to external ministry? If so, they probably need their quiet and peace when they return. Saying that married people also return from an eight-hour (or more) day does not answer the question. The vocation to marriage presupposes that the people involved find a good part of what they need in their relationship and that they care about it enough to expend time and energy upon it. And this is building for a whole future together. A husband may indeed return from a hard day and need peace and quiet, but presumably he also needs some time with his wife and children. A woman may find a day with small children wearing in the extreme—and the more so if it is half a day combined with half a day or more of work. But whatever her exhaustion, one presumes that her relationships at home are also life-giving, not death-dealing, and of primary importance in her life. Even where there is conflict, something in the life together is a source of strength; if this is not the case, something is very wrong. Nonetheless, as a married friend remarks of marriage, "One needs peace, quiet, and time to meditate to bear it [marriage]" as well. In such a life, too, the leisure for quiet is needed. Externalism or activism is equally damaging, here, though some circumstances make this a hard truth indeed. When, however, religious, unlike the married, glorify this "hardness" one begins to wonder what their values are.

In an apostolic community, the primary relationship of the religious is considered to be with God, wherever they find Him, however crucially important community and ministry may be. Even where official prayer time is restricted to half an hour in the morning, the return from the day's work needs to supply the kind of relaxation that helps the quality of life with God and others. Where, then, does community interaction fit in?

Some communities schedule prolonged times together—either a weekly meeting or some weekend time. And, of course, individuals may spend time together to deepen relationships. The difficulty, in some cases, is that where more difficult and prolonged "confrontation" (in our author's sense) needs to be done, a single weekly meeting may not suffice. Nor do people look forward to such meetings. The result can be a prolonged draining of energy in community (of which more will be said below). My own growing conviction is that the vocation to community requires the readiness to invest a certain amount of time, energy, and concern in this venture, with the corresponding readiness to decrease some of these expenditures elsewhere. Communities may need to reflect on their charism in this regard. If truly the primacy of the external ministry is such in a given vocation as to exclude this type of importance given to community, is it not, perhaps, time to reflect on whether the call to community in its contemporary form really exists?

In the case of contemplatives, the question is different. In a more silent life-style where people live closely together, it is extraordinary how much of Guggenbühl's "confrontation" occurs even without words. This can mean, however, that at some stage words will be needed to clarify misunderstandings, elucidate choices, deepen relationships. Where this does not occur, some things can fester underground and seriously hamper life with God. But readiness for such clarification may mean much talking at times. Where a habit of silence has trained people to come immediately to essentials, much can be accomplished without endless meetings. This is not always the case, however. Difficulties arise when one finds in a community one or more "communication jammers"—people with problems, complexes, or abilities to center all on themselves, preventing healthy communication among the others. And rare is the community without these! It would seem that the only solution for such situations is, once again, honesty, and then, if the community dynamic is insufficient to clear up the jamming, help from some quarter that can truly clear the blockage may be needed. Communication skills are valuable in any setting.

Guggenbühl's final observations include the idea that "marriage is not a private matter."[28] A whole larger family and net of relationships is involved. Any exclusion has the same effect as repression, for that is what it is. The same obviously holds true of community, for any community is situated in a larger world and set of interrelationships.

Finally, Guggenbühl speaks of sacrifice—and this in various domains. A marriage may not be sexually fulfilling, and this is perhaps less crucially important than one would think. One partner may have to sacrifice some gift—artistic or otherwise—to the good of the whole marriage. This sacrifice in itself may be salvific and lead more deeply toward individuation than the use of the gift. This author is quick to point out that the idea of sacrifice as a value can lead to horror and terrible deformations. Millions of young men die to gain a few feet of land, for example. And religious exaggerations along this line are well-known. Sacrifice for its own sake is not a value. But, "This does not change the fact that the sacrifice of something very dear to us appears to be indispensable for individuation, for the salvation of the soul."[29]

A psychology that rejects this idea of sacrifice can be profoundly disturbing in its effects on marriage, Guggenbühl adds, and he gives examples. The counselor who speaks only of assertiveness and self-fulfillment can destroy not only a marriage (or a community life) but also the individuation possibilities of the people involved. Guggenbühl considers the question of divorce. He does not exclude the possibility that divorce should exist but, "The criterion for whether or not to divorce should not be sought in the degree of difficulty or pathology in the marriage, but rather should clearly depend on whether or not the marriage represents for both partners a pathway of salvation."[30] What he says of divorce surely applies to community. Is community a path to salvation, to individuation? Is this *specific* community furthering the individuation of its own members? This is not a matter of sheer ease and well-being. There will be conflict as well as joy, despair as well as hope. But does the life of these people together further their growth and their life in the search for God? For if it does, then their life together, in itself and regardless of other work they do, will be helpful to others and a source of growth beyond themselves.

In summary, Guggenbühl sees marriage as a path to individuation, that is, to the coming into contact with an inner spark of divinity. He discusses the importance on this path of learning to recognize and withdraw projections in order to take one's own responsibility, and he speaks also of the importance of being able to integrate evil, suffering, the shadow, and sin. He writes of the importance of confronting the other with one's own true being, in honesty, without evasion, and without escaping from the pain of proximity. He describes the limitations people impose on each other, and speaks of the need for real sacrifice. On the positive side, he claims as important—for those called to this path—the ability to find their salvation in intensive, continuous relationship and encounter, but he points out that there is conflict as well as harmony in this process. Finally, the interest and life in this relationship are born of the ability to share who one really is, the neurotic aspects as well as the healthy, ugliness as well as beauty, the growing need for solitude as well as sharing. Here, there is life.

What does all this say to us about life in community? For one thing, it says that community is not the place of bliss and harmony that some might imagine—or try to create. If there is no conflict, no honesty, no shadow, nothing real can be built. But if I can be able to share with those around me my weakness and pain as well as my strength, my nastiness as well as my love, perhaps it is worth the struggle of a less perfect-seeming harmony.

The struggle to withdraw projections and integrate the dark aspects of reality, to find and get in touch with my own authority while recognizing that of others, the work of coming to terms with the contrasexual—within and around me—all these are necessary steps on the path toward increasing selfhood and openness to the Self deeper and greater than my own. Life together in community can help this process. But it is not an easy way.

The reflections in this chapter have thrown some light from psychology on the phenomena of marriage and community. These thoughts are seminal here and it is hoped that later chapters and cases will flesh out more of their meaning. We begin, then, in the following pages, to look at some concrete case material. Guggenbühl's thoughts and our own reflection will help us learn from these experiences.

·3·

PERSEVERANCE OR ESCAPE?

One place to apply some of the previous reflections can be found in a situation not uncommon in many forms of community life.

> A community of teaching brothers struggled at length with an internal issue. One of the group had entered out of a very disadvantaged situation, from a family with alcoholism and other problems. He found himself having to work through many personal problems and much suppressed anger. He was conscious of all of this but the quantity of built-up rage reflected on his life with his brothers. Crossing him meant weeks, if not months, of snubbing and ostracism for the guilty party. The community loved this brother, recognized his many gifts, and was concerned for his future, but felt unable to deal with the internal tension this situation caused. They also minded the weapon of silent anger. As the number of people thus targeted increased they felt the need to ask for help and to find a resolution.

This situation requires one solution for communities committed to stability and another for those that are not. The traditional "monastic" (or "stability") solution involves finding a way of dealing with the situation without any change of place for the religious in difficulty, while the solution for other communities often involves a change of community for at least some of those involved.

(As an exercise in fantasy, one ought to try to picture the above case in the situation of a women's small strictly cloistered community, for in such a situation one sees the problem at its starkest and clearest, given the limitations of size and geographical space often involved. This intensifies the emotion involved, but in fact the issues are the same in both cases.)

What is the "shadow issue" aroused by this situation? Obviously, the inner demon of anger haunts all of us. Some repress it more and others less; some face and/or express it with less trauma. But few are unconscious of its lethal potential. One is frightened to be faced with what this inner demon can do, and more frightened still to recognize it as part of oneself. Another's anger and "bad behavior" can arouse one's own, bringing a true confrontation with the shadow. And, in this case, the issue occurs in a social, community setting. What is to be done? The primary question is always one of facing and recognizing the shadow—the individual shadow and the collective shadow. But the next question is how to deal with the concrete problem.

What would be the means by which either community could deal with such a problem—especially from the perspective Guggenbühl suggests? One very important step would be efforts at personal and mutual honesty. As was said, admitting one's own anger before another's is hard, and trying to work through the issues aroused is harder still. Another step is the individual struggle of each community member to set up his or her own personal boundaries—for each to know what he or she will accept and live with and what not. And, more than once, individuals as well as the community might find themselves needing help for this. An objective observer can usually help us deal more wisely with many of these issues in ourselves and outside. Often, however, as demons resist exorcism, one finds much resistance to this step—both from the main person involved and from those who minimize or discount the issues. Just the process of looking at this need and facing it can, however, be a step toward individuation. There are, of course, other ways of taking such a step, but none that avoids the issue. The cost of dealing with all this, however, will be much pain, struggle, and psychological "work." No wonder people find themselves wanting to avoid it! One thinks of Guggenbühl's hero Culhrwch.

Let us presume, as an exercise in reflection, that the community is divided on what steps to take. The religious in question (call him Mark or her Marcia) does not want help. Some people in the house also fear the risk. Then what?

The journey of individuation is, by definition, personal. Those who feel the need for help must ask for it. Those who see the need for boundaries must struggle. And the others must follow their own light. This challenge can mean much development and maturation for individuals, even in the event that the whole community cannot work together. If all but the individual in question can, then the community can set boundaries together. This can be extraordinarily helpful toward a truly "community" solution. If the community itself is divided, then the issue becomes the growth of each individual and the steps to which that may lead. This can truly be a journey toward "salvation," individuation.

In this light, let us take a look at the "spiritual" means that have traditionally been used to deal with a case of this kind in the past. Some of these means are related to some of Guggen-bühl's suggestions. Centuries of religious have lived with the issues that arise in community and tried to deal with them in as constructive a way as they could work out, and the result has been quite a literature on the subject. Often, the encouragement has been, as above, for each person in the house to struggle and suffer toward an individual resolution of the problem.

In the sixteenth century, John of the Cross wrote:

> The first precaution is to understand that you have come to the monastery so that all may fashion you and try you. Thus, to free yourself from the imperfections and disturbances that can be engendered by the mannerisms and attitudes of the religious and draw profit from every occurrence, you should think that all in the community are artisans—as indeed they are—present there in order to prove you; that some will fashion you with words, others by deeds, and others with thoughts against you; and that in all this you must be submissive as is the statue to the craftsman who molds it, to the artist who paints it, and to the gilder who embellishes it.
>
> If you fail to observe this precaution, you will not know how to overcome your sensitiveness and feelings, nor will you get along well in the community with the religious, nor attain holy peace, nor free yourself from many stumbling blocks and evils.[1]

This means that each one tries to be loving and open and to heal whatever wounds occur in relationship without, however, great preoccupation about "relating" or, even less, about asserting himself or herself. Relationships grow where they can. In some communities, where a rule of silence was strong, people had to try to deal with these issues in an almost entirely internal way—dealing with their own inner feelings and conflicts; trying to work through to some kind of peace; knowing, often, that what happens within is conveyed nonverbally to others. For some, this struggle ended with the development of a high level of inner strength and peace—an awareness of personal boundaries, an ability not to accept inappropriate guilt feelings, a readiness to leave others their space, and an acceptance of the flaws in oneself and others without this becoming a cause for surprise or excessive pain.

For many others, however, this struggle resulted in much inner conflict, much repression of anger, many feelings of guilt and self-rejection, and much left unresolved. Partly for this reason many communities, even those with a strict rule of silence, came to the conclusion that it was important for people to be able to dialogue about their differences and questions in order to try to resolve them. This solution seems to have been helpful. But even though some misunderstandings are avoided when such exchanges are allowed, one can still trace much the same pattern as the above. The demands of life remain the same. The challenge must be faced by each individual and only then by the community. When it is thus met, such an experience can be truly salvific and individuating, as Guggenbühl would say. One could be tempted to conclude, then, that these situations are ultimately helpful for a community and the persons within it, leading each one to awareness of his or her personal shortcomings and perhaps to an awareness of a need for spiritual and/or psychological help toward a much deeper level of personal growth.

Real situations, however, confront us with other issues. Were it possible simply to grow in the personal ability to be loving, open, and free, and to hope, then, for an immediate positive result, there would be no problem. The difficulty is that, even choosing to go this route can lead to living in situations of severe conflict. People may be asked by Mark or Marcia to give up personal boundaries as far as time, attention, and freedom are concerned. Much of life can seem to be controlled by what Mark or Marcia needs or wishes and, if he or she is crossed in any way, hours of time may be needed to deal with the issues that caused anger. Once past issues are resolved, one must often avoid any further causes of anger, lest another series of explosions or verbal marathons be required. Thus life can become very difficult for community members. People can tend to avoid risking conflict because few have the time or energy necessary for such continual struggles—more time-consuming than actual psychotherapy— and so life can become constricted. A few people may have the combination of strength or firmness and outstanding leadership to be able to resist pressure and yet avoid storms. But even they often meet with only limited success. If there is a superior, some-times things can be partially eased, but only if the person in au-thority can exercise it with both strength and gentleness. And even then there is difficulty. The whole community can become in fact, largely controlled—or preoccupied—by one person. In large communities, as will be seen in a later chapter, the power of such individuals is quite limited unless they have some re-sponsibility in the house. In small groups, however, this is not the case. Is the path of salvation/individuation acceptance? Or struggle? Or more drastic means? No universal solution can be given. Here, the question is simply asked.

Centuries of religious have felt that suffering in this way was part of community living and was sanctifying. Some have even said that the more acute the pain, the closer the resemblance to Christ, who was so often misunderstood and finally betrayed by those closest to Him. In this view, the more one tries to be loving, the more one's love is purified. This can be true, but it is an effort that must be freely and consciously chosen. When it is sim-ply undergone it can be embittering and harmful. Further, this is not everyone's way. And for some who choose it as theirs, it can mean that they see love (and virtue and growth) as something totally willed. They can also pay the price of their "willing" in their bodies, often at the price of much anguish and, often, harm. The implications of such thinking and living need to be under-stood more clearly.

Another position, more common in the solitude-stressing monastic or contemplative model of community, is that inter-personal tension is secondary, unimportant, perhaps even sanc-tifying if one deals with it correctly. One can wonder, when reflecting on this view, where appropriate inner solitude or de-tachment ends and suppression or even repression of conflict begins. A general norm is impossible—but still, if the basic aim of Christian living is authentic, honest love—some conclusions about the way of relating seem required, hard as this may seem. Is not the basic Christian aim of true—that is, honest—love and peace in the house furthered more by attempting some work with the real issues, at least where this is possible? The attempt seems important.

At first glance, this whole issue seems to point to one area of contradiction between the position of classical spirituality and that of contemporary psychology. The latter would view each member of a community—even of a marriage—as having personal boundaries that ought not be sacrificed, and personal authority in relationships that is important as well. In this light, what some religious communities interpret as Christian meekness may be an abdication of fundamental, personal needs—an abdication to be paid for later by a build-up of inner tension, illness, or the inability to let oneself feel anything at all. The individual person has needs and requirements, the renunciation of which can be healthy only in certain very limited situations, where sufficient inner clarity, maturity, and freedom will not be damaged by the renunciation. In a religious context one can easily believe that one is ready to live in this way, only to find later on that the price is being paid in inner resentments that come out in all sorts of unconscious ways. And some are puzzled to learn that they are giving off messages quite different from their conscious ideals.

How can one pursue this line of reflection? Certainly one im-portant way is to encourage each individual in a problem com-munity to strive for in-depth honesty with his or her feelings. There is no way to know what is indicated for individuals or a community without this first step. A second stage would involve seeing where these experience and reflections lead. Can people deal with the pain and keep some freedom, serenity, and joy? Can life go on, or is the whole house stymied? Conclusions can grow only out of this honest and open reflection on each one's personal experience and responsibility; leaning on others is no help. And, if the issue is a common one, the reflection probably needs to be shared. Out of this sharing some conclusions may come—whether these mean continuation of the status quo, agreement that all must work together at length, or the conclusion that the present "mix" of people is impossible to continue. Any one of these conclusions can come out of a deepened inner integrity and be lived in peace—and that is the positive and purifying aspect of such conflict, difficult as it is. Deeper openness with oneself as well as with others can result.

The issue about such a situation is that this kind of in-depth reflection—on a personal and then on a community level—takes time, energy, and inner space. Many religious in active communities find themselves without these commodities—while some contemplatives find it difficult to give so much attention to "horizontal" issues. Let us deal with the first of these questions.

If a congregation sees the call to community as an important part of its charism, the fact needs to be faced that building community—like building marriage—takes time. It even requires wasting time. If people are so busy that this is impossible, perhaps community is impossible as well. I have heard surprising numbers of religious from all different kinds of communities remark that they find themselves dreading going back into the house (or, with more cloistered groups, into the community room) because of the atmosphere of unresolved conflict. In some apostolic groups, people absent themselves as much as possible, to avoid dealing with all the pain, and this is a familiar theme in marriages and families as well. An important issue, to consider, then, will be the finality and purpose of religious community, to see whether such tension is really healthy and normal, "salvific," or whether it defeats the very purpose of the group.

Many contemplative groups do indeed feel that their life is directed toward God and contemplation rather than toward the setting up of a cozy community life. This stance is obviously legitimate, but the theological and psychological question is: How can one relate appropriately to God if one does not relate appropriately to oneself and others? The relating subject is one and the same. Is not my relatedness to self and others the training ground for my relationship with God (the "active life" of early ascesis that prepares for the contemplative), as well as vice versa? There is a profound reason for the statement that the two commandments of love are one. If a person cannot relate, either his or her contemplation or its human foundations seem suspect—though it is equally false to think relating replaces contemplation.

Are there any alternatives to the attempt to struggle toward individual clarity, honesty, and strength, and then toward a common solution to the problem? If there are, I do not know them. The question is: where would such a "common solution" lead? As individuals grow in strength, the community may be able to carry its problem together and work with it positively. Or the solution for some individuals—in a congregation that does not strive for stability within each community—might be to leave the community. Or the solution might be that Mark or Marcia would need to get help if he or she wishes to stay. Christian communities and religious tend to shrink from drastic solutions, fearing them as a lack of love. But Guggenbühl's question remains: Is this being together furthering salvation/individuation for those involved? If there is growth, one can hope so. If there is only suffering, is the suffering salvific? Some would answer, "Potentially, yes." But perhaps part of the potential is precisely that some suffering can lead to a choice to live in other ways. Once again, each individual's path is his or her own.

What solutions are appropriate for communities committed to stability? Here people must work with the issues knowing that changing house or asking another to do so is only a very extraordinary and perhaps impossible solution. What is to be done? In a small cloistered group, chronic conflict with one or more very difficult or troubled personalities can lead in some cases to a pathology of the whole. An entire community can become affected by the pathology of one that others are not strong enough to resist. In some cases the choice between individual and common sickness and health does require facing the problem with great honesty and getting help. Suspicion of current psychological practice—while often justified for contemplatives—can lead to the opposite error of fearing all help. Surely someone with appropriate insights can be found. The process can be upsetting but it can also lead to a real clarification of individual and common goals and beliefs, to an understanding of the human bases of prayer. The community can be helped to move toward an appropriate and lucid solution of the problem. To know that such solutions do exist—even if some may seem drastic or frightening—is important: they are better than nonsolutions.

In "nonstable" communities, again, one solution has been an annual move for some people with problems. In one sense, pressure is thus taken off both communities and individuals. The problem is, of course, that where this means is used through the years, the real problem of both the individual and of the individual community members may never be addressed. People can go through decades without being faced with their shortcomings or the effect these have on others and on themselves. Community members may also fail to touch their own weakness. In this sense, the lack of stability in a congregation's structure can be both a help to problem solving and a means of escape from really looking at actual problems. Cloistered communities do not have this facility, but they can avoid facing issues through a kind of fatalism, as well as through fear of seeing. Again, a false understanding of charity in both situations can lead to false harmony, where volcanoes are surging under the surface, both in the group and in the individual. Problems that have not been faced can grow to incurable proportions.

After all this reflection, one must remember that we live in the real world. Not everyone is healthy, and almost no one completely so. Not all ills can be cured, and no situation is perfect. One deals with the possible and never the perfect. But it is important to know that the possible may be better than one thought.

One final commentary on this case needs to be made. The case presented involved "cold anger," but the dynamics of "hot anger" in a community are much the same. It is possible in some cases— even more frequent, perhaps, than those of "cold anger"—for an entire community or house to be controlled by one person's habit of temper outbreaks when displeased. Heredity, environment, ethnic considerations, and personality type all play a part here. In some circles or for some temperaments, a temper tantrum is a one-moment thing, forgotten immediately afterward. But normally the forgetting is done more by the perpetrator who has gotten his or her feelings out of his system, rather than by those on the receiving end, who often—in the interests of avoiding a total scene—have not. In some ethnic groups all such manifestations are taken more in stride than in others, but even in these situations, anger can become a powerful weapon. The dynamics, as a result, are not very different from the ones mentioned above.

As a final exercise before concluding this chapter, let us take our original case study as a "sacred space," a dream, a symbolic expression of an inner world or reality. In one sense, all dream interpretation is subjective, so that one cannot say what such an episode would "mean" on a universal level. In another sense, however, one can say that a given dream for a given person does have a meaning that is real and can be known by others. Case material can be helpful in much the same way. For the community above, then, what could the experience mean?

The first issue is one of struggle—a "salvation theme" par excellence, as Guggenbühl pointed out. St. George conquers the dragon; Culhrwch perseveres through blood, grime, and ordeals to find his love. Having to struggle toward a common solution can be a healthy and salvific experience.

In the case cited at the beginning of this chapter, one of the group came out of a suffering home situation that left him with unresolved issues of anger. This leads to a confrontation with shadow material, with the problems of injustice and evil, with the personal "dragon" for both the brother concerned and the community. Because the brother's own struggle has not been moving toward a more integrating conclusion, his own shadow material becomes that of the whole community. They must all deal with it in him; they are all called to battle. If they answer the call, this will be growth producing for him as well. Where they do not, it is their own areas of weakness in dealing with this shadow that are expressed.

One can conclude, then, that the situation is indeed salvific in that it is a challenge to struggle and deal with forces needing integration. The anger that could be a source of health and power used for good becomes shadow by its repression or its unsuitable and unintegrated use. The community "felt unable to deal with the internal tension" aroused. The image is almost one of internal flood waters rising in the house and submerging the inhabitants. The unconscious is often depicted in images of water, and anger unresolved becomes as unconscious as its roots.

What is the meaning of this mounting tension or flood? Basically, it expresses the community's sense of powerlessness. And when one feels powerless before events, one needs help—the fairy tale's wizard, the godmother, the magic charm. The "outside help" of a therapist can seem such a charm, but the help thus afforded is valuable only if it helps the people concerned find their own inner resources. "They also minded the weapon of silent anger." In mythological or dream language, a weapon must be met by another weapon or an equal power of some sort. And this weapon or power must be the beleaguered person's own to use: that is to say, it must come from within. It must provide strength to oppose and refuse manipulation—wherever this refusal may lead. Bloody battle is a part of myths, fairy tales, and dreams. It cannot be refused any more in real life than in fiction. The call of this situation to the individuals concerned is a call to battle—primarily interior—to avoid flight.

"They felt the need to ask for help and to find a resolution." The result of increased help and strength, then, was to be a "resolution," a coming to some sort of peace, to the octave note on the scale. Perhaps this would mean the attacker had to be routed—the inner issues far more than the external person. But the external problems need appropriate handling as well. This seems the only way to "resolution." It does not mean the cessation of anger in the angry person. Rather, it means the need to find an appropriate way to deal with this anger and its causes, for the individual, and a collective way to work appropriately with the issue and what it shows.

This sacred or mythological space obtained by casting this whole case in a mythological or symbolic mode translates the story, then, into one of battle with evil forces. Anger is a power within us with which we need to come to terms—individually and collectively. It is not in itself evil but its misuse can make it so. Strength is needed for this process—and honesty—but the growth of these powers furthers individuation. The community, in such difficult situations, also becomes a testing ground for central individuation issues: anger and evil, resolution and peace, weakness and strength, evasion and truth.

·4·

SHALOM

The Shalom community is composed of four religious from a teaching community, all now in their seventies. Three were active in university teaching and writing—the latter remaining still one of their activities—and one in provincial administration, where she still works. They long remained active in their neighborhood, in a university town, though health reasons lead them to decrease this activity now. They refer to their present experience as "the tremendous grace of living in this community" and have considerable impact on novices and prospective vocations who meet them as a group. They are profoundly happy in their life together, though they admit having had to work through to their present situation. Three of the present group of four have lived together in small community for nine years.

The idyllic picture presented in the above case leads one to the desire to investigate further. Is the situation truly as successful as it seems? What was the price of this success? To what do those involved attribute their success? Is it repeatable or is it a unique formula applicable only to this specific group of people? All these questions led me to request a prolonged interview with the whole group, even after speaking with some individuals in it.

Asked to what they attribute the success of their arrangement, they spoke first of what they called a "natural substratum" of common temperament, experience, and age. Three of the group

50

had worked in the same university for some time before retiring and there had been friendship even then.

The three who had been together the longest felt their similarity in age to be a very positive factor. "It is lonely to be the only one of one's age in a community. [This remark came from experience.] It is relaxing to be with one's contemporaries." The most recent addition to the group, a sister still active in administration, had more doubts than the others on this point, and perhaps more fear of losing touch with the thought of younger groups in the congregation. This may be partly because her work gives her less contact with, for example, the groups of novices who come to seminars with the other three. It may also be partly because of her more recent experience with other communities of more mixed ages. This group feels that they would be willing to be mixed with a group of other ages if there were at least three people in the latter group sufficiently contemporary with each other, but not if there were fewer. "It would be too hard for them."

Another factor they stress as a cause for the harmony of their lives is their respect for each other's needs for quiet. They once had someone wish to join the group who was on a different wavelength in this regard. After some experience of their life she decided of her own volition not to ask to join them. While they do not spell out their life-style in so many words, they are clear that there is a continuum between solitude and togetherness and that their desires along these lines are similar, with a rather strong bias toward solitude. This does not, however, prevent frequent and warm interaction, not only in the community but with others. But the source of this warmth seems to lie to a large degree in a certain sureness that the needed quiet will be safeguarded. They remark that the similarity in age means similar religious training and similar experience of religious life. So, similarity of expectations makes for a certain ease in their establishment of life patterns. "We agree on basic values," they say.

Asked how much of their success as a community has to do with the rather unique personal gifts of the community members, one remarked that she would attribute it more to the fact of their being mentally very active. "We know what is going on. We are interested and have time to pursue our interests." Having worked on a college level they have managed to keep in touch with a certain number of former students and former interests. They are always open to new interests as well. The fact of their continuing to write is no doubt a further help.

Their very specific rhythm and life-style are important, however. They are aware of their impact as a group and say that part of it is attributable to their being able to live a common life-style. "We have a slower pace. We don't stay up late or attempt to go to movies. We can do what we do *because* we live a moderate rhythm." These observations were partly a reflection on the advantages of not having younger members in the group. It would doubtless be far more tiring to have to live with others going at a faster pace, they say. Still, "some of the younger want a quiet life, too," one remarked, while another spoke of the general noise level in much of even religious community life today and the importance of its effects.

Theological issues are involved. One person remarked that the decision of communities formerly of "mixed life," like this one, to call themselves "apostolic" led to a whole period when people were always trying to be "inserted in the world," when there was a constant stream of outsiders coming in, and life became exhausting. Some of this has subsided, they say, and their community does not live this way—despite its very real openness, hospitality, and warmth of welcome. But the theological issues underlying these questions seem to need reflection—even as to their human basis. One can be so "apostolic" that one burns out, individually and collectively. The remark was made that this experience was not a question of age, that even novices seemed to mind when their house became a hotel and the comings and goings were too frequent. "That is disrupting. It is promising that they mind."

The question of communities of mixed age arose again. If a small community is to remain small, one person remarked, how could it include several people of each age group? And where contemporaries are lacking, one can be too lonely. This statement was made again, after the previous discussion on this point, and was based on experience. It seems a strong conviction here.

Another person returned to the question of intellectual capacity. Life used to be structured in a way that helped people with less intellectual power, she remarked. There was reading in common and at meals; there were common events in the day of any larger community. Now people need to be able to "go it" on their own. If there is not sufficient intellectual capacity, even more than spiritual, perhaps, life is hard in the present structures—or lack thereof. This raises serious issues about formation today.

Asked their feelings about small communities as opposed to large, almost all expressed their relief and happiness with present developments. "It is a relief to be a small group, sharing in the work of the house," remarked one—and then added that work requiring much travel and constant relating with new groups was very tiring.

All four spoke of the importance of considerateness—sharing information, respecting others' needs for space and others' feelings on various levels. The need for simple human manners to facilitate peaceful relating was another remark from all.

How do they handle tensions and disagreements? One remarks that she tries to forget it but does something for the other person, rather than apologize. Another says that any tensions in the house—even those of others—are difficult for her, but a third says that in all their years together there have been only three times of really major tension. "I learned how to handle conflict under the old system," says one. But, they added, with increasing years one becomes more moderate, more civilized, more able to relativize, more aware of what is not worth bothering about.

Asked if there are any further points they would like to mention, they spoke once again of the need of guaranteeing for everyone the quiet needed for prayer and mentioned specifically the fact that, although their apartment is tiny, the television can be used in a place others cannot hear—even though they use it little and at limited times. They mentioned the difficulty of living with people who are very insensitive to sound, and remark that they share this sensitivity. "If quiet were absent, it would be terrible."

They speak also, however, of the conclusions that follow if a religious order sees community as an essential part of its ethos. "If community is that important, some other things may have to yield." They mentioned specifically in this regard an undue concern for economizing. Things that are needed for the building up of a sane community life are not the ones that should be done without, even in the interests of poverty or economy.

Finally, they say, "We chose each other. We shared the same basic hopes, the same emphasis on quiet, prayer, order, cleanliness," and many common interests. Their mutual choice certainly seems to have borne beautiful fruit.

When one reflects on the experience of community these four religious represent, certain questions arise. For one thing, the group seems composed of people with many personal, intellectual, and spiritual gifts. Would not such a group always succeed? Has its success anything to do with the dynamics of community in general?

My own reflection on these points made me skeptical in the beginning. It seemed to me that most people would be glad to live with any one of these four women and that therefore their experience together would not show much of universal importance. But more thought and discussion brought other conclusions. These women may be attractive and agreeable but no one of them would be willing to live in just any group and, if she were honest about her needs, almost any one of them could fairly make demands of some groups that would be difficult to meet. That is to say that there seems to be real wisdom in their view that harmony is born of a certain compatibility of age, experience, interest, life rhythms. They are not trying to be all things to all people. They are being themselves individually and collectively and have set up a common life where they can do this. And the experience is positive, for their natural rhythms fit well together, and they are not trying to force themselves into some contemporary mode that is not truly theirs. And, paradoxically, by being themselves in their age group and with their rhythm, they relate beautifully with the young—the same young they might find it a great strain to live with in a small community.

They are also aware that they are far from wanting the lifestyle some of their contemporaries might want or need. Much talking, much entertainment, and much activity are not important to them, and they would find it a strain to live with someone who needed these. They have known their inner tensions and, despite their courtesy and restraint, they have been honest about these. They know what they want and who they are and are able to share this.

It is good that their order encouraged them to live what they are living and did not force them into some other mold or mixture that might theoretically seem better by virtue of offering a variety of ages or some other apparent value. The real value here seems to flow from what this group sensed as important for itself, individually and together.

Their apartment is tiny—too tiny, some would think. The area where they live is very simple and unassuming. There is a real choice of simplicity in much that they do, but this seems something of which they are hardly aware, they do it so naturally. One wonders if they had to move what they would choose, but it would very likely be more of the same. It does not seem that they fall into essential choices by accident.

On the concrete level, before discussing the symbolic, what seems to be the lesson of this particular experience?

Partly, there is the importance of mutual selection based on a certain amount of self-knowledge and experience of one's needs. One wonders if superiors could have assigned a group so well without the mutual choice of the members.

Then there is the issue of life-style. This group knows its needs, shares the same priorities, respects each other's values and does not really want members on other wavelengths. This point seems very important.

The fact of common training and expectations, a common spirituality, is important. That members belong to the same order does not at all imply a totally identical spirituality or identical gifts. Living with others who share the same values in daily life is a successful experience in this case.

The firmness of this group on the importance of being with others of the same age bears reflection. It flies in the face of much that is being said today, and perhaps is all the more important for that reason. Less than three of an age, they feel, is too few. Interesting.

It is essential to ask once more about the apparently ideal nature of this scene. Is there nothing negative in this picture? The four involved would say of course. There are always the little struggles, disagreements, and sensitivities of daily life. And they are aware of having had moments and times of difficulty. But their present situation is truly happy. Some psychologists might consider that their accents on manners, courtesy, and mutual respect could mean that some things need to be more frankly shared and are not. This may be true. But I am not sure the end product does not bear out the wisdom of their choice. If they had to deal with someone truly difficult, I do not know what their choice would be—whether they would deal with it by silence and courtesy and wait for a change or whether they would be, while still very courteous, very frank as well. Knowing the group as I do, I suspect their choice would be frankness. Their writing and conversation suggest as much. But this question must be left to conjecture for the present. The relevance of some of their observations for other groups—marriages, families, or larger— seems obvious, despite the unique character of this group. Their experience speaks for itself.

A final reflection on the experience of community for single age groups seems in order. We have all heard many tales very far from this peace and joy. One truly essential point seems the cultivation of personal interests, skills, hobbies—intellectual, manual, artistic, relational. Nothing is sadder than a group of retired or semiretired women or men rattling around in a house miserably sharing some gossip or constant television but without any apparent aim. But personal interests or relational skills are not developed at the age of seventy. Asking—or encouraging— the sacrifice of such gifts in the young can easily lead to their becoming dried up and empty with greater age. The point is of prime importance: the inability to relate in some older people living together is truly saddening and thought provoking.

This said, let us reflect on the whole experience symbolically, entering into the "space" of this experience of community living as one would enter into a fairy tale, a symbolic story, or a dream. To begin, one must face the fact that there is something rather magical and enchanted about this "space." I have called this chapter "Shalom" for a reason. I have brought visitors of various ages—from their twenties to their seventies—to visit this group, and the reaction has always been, "What an experience! What women!" There is, then, a magic in this set of people—which perhaps implies that what is possible for this group might not be easily generalizable. For the present, however, let us remain in this enchanted space and give in to the enchantment.

These women, in fairy-tale language, are "wise women," wisdom figures. They are over seventy; they show the effects of years of experience from which they have learned. But their house is not only a place of wisdom but also one of humility. It is small and quite poor, in an unassuming neighborhood. The plot on which the house stands is small and another family lives in the other half of the house. This poverty, in the fairy-tale world, often goes with wisdom.

As a place of humility, it is also, in terms of the Christian mythology, a place of charity and, I would suspect, of healing as a result. These women receive many visitors with love and respect—people of all kinds. They are concerned with their neighborhood and its activities. One receives from them a feeling not of separation but of participation in the life around them, and one meets among their visitors intellectuals and sufferers, the poor and the rich. They seem to care—and that is often a source of healing. So we find ourselves in a fairy-tale house, in a poor part of the city, where there live four wise women to whom people come for the experience of love, healing, and happiness they find in this magic house. For happiness is part of what these four wise women mention in the "tremendous grace" of being together. But their stories speak of the struggles they have gone through, individually and collectively, to reach this place and this situation of peace. The life of this "magic house" is the fruit of a long quest—or, rather, of four long quests, intertwined and separate, which have borne this common fruit.

What has all this fairy-tale lyricism to say to us? Does it not sound almost unreal? It does, but this may be because it speaks of something rare—the combined fruit of four lives, four sets of choices, four processes of individuation, which combine as something more than the sum of the parts. Each of these women alone would have less to give than the combination of the four together. Much of the "magic" is born of the chemistry of this particular combination, which they themselves chose. Once again, then, this emphasizes the blessed results of mature choice.

Would the fairy-tale be the same if they lived in a palace? I think not. The smallness and simplicity of the house has something to do with the magic. It speaks. It is part of what they share. Perhaps it is part of the happiness.

So, to move toward a conclusion, where would one find the source of the magic? In the individuality of the people, first of all. They have reached it themselves but they value and further it in each other. If the uniqueness of each individual is something precious, one finds it here. One must say sadly that not all communities of religious have this kind of magic. Some, on the contrary, seem to crush the individuality, freedom, and joy of their members—not because there is any intention of doing so but because some strong personalities can override some weak ones or some less sensitive override those more so, and people have not always learned how to fight these battles and take their own strength in hand appropriately. And so evil can seem to triumph over good, even in a place where the basic ethos spoken of is one of love. This last issue warps the scene still further because words and aims then contradict real experience, and people go through all sorts of internal contortions trying to work out this contradiction. In the Shalom community, love and mutual respect and individuality are well lived, though perhaps with less confrontation than Guggenbühl mentions. Even so, the interactions are very real and thus this fairy-tale space speaks of healing and of health.

If I met these four wise women in a dream, I think their message to me would be the same—the importance of truly living the human journey of individuation, of moving toward wisdom. Judging from others' reactions to them, they seem to bear this message to many people. These women speak by their lives of human development and growth, which are inseparable from spiritual growth and progress. I believe that much in the humility of their lives and setting, even the humility of accepting increasing age and ill health very simply, are part of what prevents the note of inflation such a group could easily develop.[1] They are gifted, cultivated, and attractive. It would have been easy for them to be other than humble, to try to deny what the increasing years may mean. But rather, they accept. And that, too, is wisdom.

In a sense, to speak of them collectively is foolish. Four very different personalities, with very different areas of attractiveness and possible annoyance, lend themselves little to "grouping." But we are speaking here of a community more than of individuals. I am sure any one of the four could be unattractive at times, each in a different way. But where there is no shadow, there is no real light.

Let us return, then, more completely from the world of magic to daily reality and ask what the fairy tale has taught us about community. I believe that its lesson concerns the value of the human journey toward individuation and the value of people who have made this journey in communities. They need not always be highly educated or full of artistic gifts. We have surely all met some of the simplest of people who were also the most individuated or wise.

Any one person who is making this journey seriously is a boon in a community. A group of such people is even more so. And perhaps this is the crux of many contemporary problems about community. A series of problem people form a problem community. A group of people with much unintegrated material will produce a community carrying the sum total of that material. It is foolish to expect that such a situation could be harmonious.

Certain monastic or contemplative structures facilitate dealing with this material, since elements like silence and solitude and spiritual help of various kinds (if it is honest with the human in people) can be very useful. Where these are lacking, coming to terms with much inner material can be difficult. But when silence, solitude, and structure are misused—not intentionally, but through ignorance—the worst can be the corruption of the best. Once again, wisdom and often guidance are important.

Active, or apostolic, communities have different advantages. The tests and situations of life can bring to the fore many inner issues that could otherwise remain hidden, and the freedom of relationships can make it easier to work through some of these issues. But the essential is having the necessary inner space to deal with all this appropriately. Otherwise, here, too, what might have been opportunity can become simply exacerbation of problems that already exist. And these compound in community, unless people learn how to struggle with them, unless there are members who understand—who, in other words, fight or have fought the dragons.

Shalom community speaks to us, then, of the importance of individual wisdom, realism, integration—and humility. And its community living speaks of the importance of each brick in the edifice and its strength. Anything that helps even one is a help to the whole. Building something of value at a lesser price does not seem possible.

·5·

POWER

A small community of religious priests runs a parish in the center of the country, far from most of the communities of the order. They have chosen not to have a superior, though one is designated pastor. This latter is a young priest with very considerable charm and sophistication and also with very considerable leadership and power over the others. The community contains one or two men who are his friends and largely follow his lead. It also contains one or two others who have been assigned there and who feel like outsiders. They not only do not belong to the leading group, but they also have almost no part in the decision making. Being older or shy and less educated, they take no firm stand on these points but are very unhappy. The order frequently has to transfer such members of the community.

The issue here is not particularly subtle. It involves the influence of one strong personality in a group, notably when that group has no named authority. Study of groups shows that when no one is named to an authority position in a group, the group throws up its own leader—whether the most gifted or, at times, the most manipulative. If the group were to choose an official leader, the same person might well be chosen, but in this case the person becomes accountable to some higher authority or at least to the group. When the leadership remains wholly unofficial, this is not the case.

The obvious issue in these dynamics is less the "following" spirit of members two and three (call them Secundus and Tertius). Rather the unhappiness of numbers four and five—Quartus and

61

Quintus—is the problem. In our age of psychological awareness, one might be tempted to say, "Well, all they have to do is learn to be a little more assertive and personal." But Quartus and Quintus are not young men. Quartus is not particularly well educated, and Quintus is very timid and shy. Community life being what it is, their lives can be overrun to quite a serious degree by the younger group. Their access to cars, money, and community facilities is decided by the leadership group, and often in what seems to the others a truly tyrannical way. Their own oversensitivity makes this situation worse and makes them unable to take a firm position. The provincial, when he visits, encourages them to be more forthright, but he does not want to do their work for them by remonstrating with the others.

One ends, then, with a situation in which, out of five people, two are very unhappy and often resentful; two are basically simply followers; and one runs the group. It is easy to be condemnatory about this last person, Primus, but it is hardly his fault if no one stands up to him. He is intelligent enough to see what his position in the group is, but he sees no reason to encourage others to use their own authority when they are not naturally so inclined. He is not heavily into psychology, nor is he very sensitive to what others may feel. In fact, he can be quite verbally devastating when crossed, and this is part of what makes him feared.

Secundus and Tertius feel no need for help. Quartus and Quintus often express their unhappiness to others of their order when they meet them, and, more than once, they have been told that it is up to them not to allow themselves to be "steamrollered." But they find this a hard saying. Finally, they, like many before them, ask to be transferred.

The provincial now faces a quandary. Given their age and temperament, should he accede to their request? Should he tell them to resist the power of the others and, if necessary, get help to do so? Or should he speak to Primus, and possibly Secundus and Tertius, about the situation? He finally decides to speak to the whole community together to try to clarify things, but at the meeting Quartus and Quintus are not ready to say much more than that they are not happy and wish to move. (It is worth noting that in communities with somewhat parallel situations, I know of more than one case where the person leaving even said publicly, "It is no one's fault but mine that I'm not happy"—a very true statement in one way but a means of not giving the facts in another. People sometimes express problems clearly in private and clam up in public—where a solution could be sought—often to the despair of the few who do have courage to speak.)

The ball is in the provincial's court. If he makes the older men stay, he is trying to use them to form the younger group as well as themselves—if they can reach that level of strength after much pain. But he is also not honoring their considered request to move. This may be an individuating situation for them and for the others, but this will only be the case if Quartus and Quintus are able to choose and will it as such, rather than feeling simply victimized and resentful at a negative answer to their request. It will also only be the case if and when they become strong enough to resist the power of the other group and to brave the friction involved in resisting. For older men, this is not easy—perhaps not possible.

The provincial could also send in someone else who is strong and who has some clarity concerning the issues, but he has no one to spare at present. If he chooses to speak to the younger group, he infantilizes the older ones and can only hope for an improvement in the situation if Primus himself is willing to try to be more aware of the others. But this is not one of his gifts or desires. He is, further, very busy in the parish. This serves as an excellent reason to avoid internal dynamics in the house. In the end, the provincial decides, in the interests of peace, to let the older men move and to be careful whom he sends to the house, knowing that he may need to change people there frequently. The result of this decision will be, of course, that Primus becomes stronger and the other four, in their different ways, weaker, but the provincial sees no alternative.

Is there an alternative? Much depends on the stance both of the provincial and of the community—not to speak of the order as a whole. If community is seen as simply a place to live while carrying out a ministry—a place that one hopes will be relatively peaceful and relaxing—then everyone involved is likely to take the line of least resistance, and perhaps rightfully so. If their apostolic work takes almost the whole of their energy and forms the essence of their vocation, then it is important to be able to come home and relax.

On the other hand, if community life is also part of this particular vocation with its own place in the mission of the community—if, in other words, it is a religious community in the full sense of that term, rather than an institute of clerics gathered simply for ministry—then it seems that the living of community is in itself a value with its own right and demands, which again requires a certain expenditure of time, energy, and reflection; it cannot simply be taken for granted. Community does not just happen by itself when a certain number of people live under one roof as in a hotel or boarding house. It takes effort, time, and work. Relationships are part of it, and a common thrust of some kind as well. These things do not just happen by themselves, nor do they continue to live without any cultivation, whether in marriage, families, or religious groups.

One essential question is whether and how often the community meets and how much in-depth, sincere relating happens at these meetings. A community business meeting to settle concrete details of life may happen regularly without giving much if any support to real community building. Only if people share real feelings, hopes, concerns, and pains can such meetings truly build the interrelationships of community. The community in our case rarely met in this way.

The still deeper question involves the purpose of community. Is it truly meant to further individuation/salvation? If it is, then a provincial decision leading all sides to a less individuating result would run counter to the very purpose of community itself. On the other hand, the individuation process comes out of the person himself or herself, not from an authority. If the members of this community were to use their situations as a means toward growth, they would have to choose for themselves to further this end. For Quartus and Quintus to make this choice would mean a free decision to try to grow in strength and to find the necessary support where they can. Since the other three are not hurting, they may not feel impelled toward any particular choice, at least until Quartus and Quintus begin to act and to speak. When they do so, their increased openness and strength may become a means of increasing insight for the others as well as for themselves. One could hope this situation might eventually be more salvific for all. One must not, however, minimize the cost for the older two. Hence a decision to stay would have to be their free choice, not something they consider wholly beyond their strength and desires. It is also difficult to imagine their not needing help in the process, and the other three might well resist a "facilitator."

There are reasons why Quartus and Quintus might not elect to stay and struggle. Fatigue, stress, a need for peace, and other such reasons might be very valid for older men not ready to take on such a struggle in community. Many religious, male and female, have chosen to live alone for just such reasons, rather than continue the hassle and conflict of community life. It cannot be said that they are not pursuing their individuation. They may just be pursuing it in a different way. Whether they wish to be honest about their reasons for departure is, however, a question of real importance for those they leave behind.

The whole issue connects with a related and very important one. If one looks closely at a series of communities of one's own acquaintance and relates the degree of happiness or unhappiness of the members to the degree and kind of leadership or power in the house, I suspect one will come out with some rather interesting conclusions. My own impression is that situations of leadership or power (or rather, the people who have it) are divided into two rough categories: one where power is habitually wielded in a way helpful to and harmonious with the whole and everyone's good, and the other where there is or has been a history where power has been used unhelpfully for the whole. One often finds that the happiness or harmony of the community as a whole can depend largely on the use of this particular gift of leadership or power.

I am aware that this conclusion would seem to conflict with this book's stress on individuation. But I believe that this contradiction is only apparent. Social psychology's description of a pecking order, in which every fowl is either pecker or pecked, though its role may be different in a different dyad, has become a standard image of our culture. In communities, too, there are leaders and followers, though a leader in one situation may be a follower in another and although there are different forms and areas of leadership. Still, roughly speaking, some have more power in a house and some less; and, others experience this power as either positive or negative.

My suggestion is that the existence of positive power in a community is a bonus not to be ignored in the construction of community. And the existence of negative power is something to be very seriously reckoned with, and seen with concern. Negative power can be a result of personal unsolved conflict which, once resolved, can become force for good. Or it can simply point to a negative conjunction of membership in a group. It can, obviously, be a stimulus to much serious work toward individuation on the part of people who suffer from its effects, and such work can be helpful both to them and to the person with the power. Nonetheless, the issue needs to be addressed and considered, doubtless more than in the case of people with less leadership, for its ramifications effect all concerned.

As was just said, the other and equally important side of the coin is that of the follower, or the "pecked." An unhappy follower also spreads unhappiness, though less than a leader. A happy "follower" can have far more influence for good than he or she knows. The term *happiness,* however, is superficial in this context, for the real issue is not so much happiness or contentedness as the kind of integration that makes someone a positive influence in a group. "Followers" can lead in this way. The conclusion is, then, that any personal unsolved issues will ripple out to the farthest edges of a group or family, especially when they are present in someone with more power. In the best of all possible worlds everyone in a group would be so individuated that other people's power or problems would have only minor effects on others. This is, however, not a wholly realistic expectation. To be impervious to the people with whom one lives is to be distanced, internally if not externally. If community is meant to be life giving, one would hope that such distancing would not be necessary.

This leaves each person living with others with a double challenge: that of dealing with personal material for the sake of others as much as oneself, and that of becoming sufficiently free of others' power to live one's own life. And finally, there is the collective challenge of taking together the time and trouble to work through issues needing attention for the sake of the whole.

In the setting of a community, marriage, or other group, questions of social psychology cannot be neglected with impunity. The issue of power, positive or negative, is a reality that needs to be seriously faced, not denied, as is so often the case. For the inner construction of common living is not a phenomenon that occurs without the strong influence of power and the need to integrate this major element.

What, then, is the shadow in this particular case or struggle? Another's power and one's own reaction to it can make one aware of cowardice and weakness. One's own power can cause fear of being a steamroller and can lead some people to cease being themselves—ostensibly for the sake of others. But this is not the solution. Rather, the shadow needs to be faced. Weakness and power are not "demons" but essential questions to face on the journey. Groups of children in a family or school, people in a working situation, couples—all face this dynamic. It is part of the human struggle.

Let us transpose this whole case onto the level of a dream or fairy tale and see what it yields. In a fairy-tale situation, Primus would doubtless become the king and Secundus and Tertius his knights. Quartus and Quintus are unhappy in this kingdom, where others have power and they are weak. They need to deal with their problem as the crux of the tale.

One way would be by leaving the scene of their misery, either by an inner growth in strength or by a journey elsewhere. Perhaps they will meet a dwarf, a dragon, or a fairy who will give them some magic object to supply them with strength. Perhaps they will find the bluebird of happiness in their own backyard, as in Maeterlinck's tale, and then the king will not matter. Or perhaps they will need to go on pilgrimage to find their place of peace. In the Grimm fairy tale "Three Feathers," the Dumling who will become the future king finds the solutions for all his challenges by going deeper where he is—by going down into the ground where he finds the toad who can give him the magic answers.

What, in real life, would be the magical solution or the strengthening potion? Who would be the wizard or fairy who helps find it, or who the dragon? The former could be a counselor, therapist, director, or friend ready to work with these men toward their own greater honesty and strength. The dragon could be their own inner fears and resistances, which, once conquered, make external battles seem easy in comparison. Their real issue is the "shadow" of their own weakness or fear which they must overcome to find peace.

But Primus himself has his own struggle. He is not the fairy-tale king under whom the land prospers. To learn the beneficent use of power he will have his own journey to make, as will Secundus and Tertius if they, too, are to individuate and not just be followers forever.

What does this tale say about the case we have just discussed? First, that the acceptance of subservience out of weakness is bad for the soul. Second, that the journey toward strength is incumbent upon the sufferer but that he or she can find help. Third, that such suffering may be a grace toward individuation. Fourth, that, once helped, the one suffering will be strong enough to live more peacefully and without feeling so "invaded" or controlled by another's strength. He or she will be able to allow another to have power without losing all of his or her own. And fifth, that power itself is a "talent" in the biblical sense: it needs work if it is to be used wisely. One is not simply born a "good king" without effort. This issue is a very important one in communities and families, and this case speaks of some of the asperities of the road toward power's appropriate use.

·6·

PARADOX AND DISCERNMENT

Sacred Heart Monastery is a small community in the rural Midwest. At first glance it would seem that the odds are against this group. The building is not beautiful; it used to be a school and was bought by the community because they could afford nothing else. It has been more or less adapted to community living, but in many places the paint is coming off the walls and the roof needs repair—not for lack of ability to care for these things but for lack of funds and materials.

In the years after Vatican II almost all of the younger members left. One would have expected the community to die out but, almost miraculously, some new young people began to show interest. Today the community comprises five very elderly monks; two of middle age—one borrowed from another community and serving as novice master—and three novices. Two of these latter show real promise and attachment to the life and to the community which they have entered, but, as with any novitiate, they still need to stand the test of time.

There is only one priest in the house at present, beside the novice master, and he is the prior—an elderly but very saintly and learned man, much loved by all but frail in health. As a means of livelihood, the group does a certain amount of translation work and a bit of farming; also, a few guests come for retreats and occasionally leave substantial offerings. The community manages to eat and keep minimally warm but not much else.

Judging superficially, one would say, "a dying community." Yet retreatants speak of the peace and beauty they find in this house, and the novices speak with enthusiasm of the future. "It will never be a large or impressive community," one says, "but the love and peace and joy in the house make me very happy here. Yes, the community is old, even very old. But we hope to learn from them and carry on in their footsteps."

Spending time with this group is instructive. Since the novices are still learning the life, all the major jobs in the house are carried on by the old monks. One has charge of the farm—which is mostly a few cattle—and he does what he can quietly and peacefully. Another takes care of the monks' clothing and all the laundry for them and the guests, with the help of a novice for the heavier chores. He is a man who in any other walk of life would be retired and, no doubt, feeling useless. Here he works from morning to night but at a rhythm suited to his strength and without too much strain. He is happy to experience his usefulness and does not usually feel the need for extra rest.

A third older monk takes care of the liturgy and the guests. The former job is a large one in a monastic community: it involves choosing texts, hymns, and books for an activity that takes some hours each day. The latter involves caring for the guests' rooms and needs—including spiritual direction, if required. A fourth monk is infirm and needs almost full-time care from a middle-aged brother, who also cares for the cooking, with a novice's help.

One might think it all sounds too peaceful, despite the amount of physical work involved, but there are strains. The age of the community means much fatigue and can lead to anxiety—or could if they let it. Will they be able to continue the recitation of the Hours, which is their very life? Will they be able to continue earning their living? Even now there is just barely enough to cover food and minimal heating and they habitually wear all the wool they can in winter to reduce heating costs. There is no question of electric fans, let alone air conditioning, in the very hot summers, though some of the older men are not well. Will the novitiate continue to recruit? No one has asked for information for two years and the present group of novices is almost ready for profession, though one is not entirely happy and may not persevere. What is the outlook for the future?

The serenity and wisdom of the prior are one element that greatly helps the peace of the whole. His leadership, though discreet, is strong, and his refusal to lose himself in anxiety about the future helps the whole group to continue with considerable trust. The revival of the novitiate seems to show that this trust is appropriate, and the presence of the younger men gives the place an air of new life. The novice master, questioned as to his prognosis for the future, remarks that prophecy is not his gift. No one could have predicted the arrival of this younger group; no one can know what the future will bring. He wishes to train the younger men to continue with courage and believe that they will be guided. Perhaps, with time, one of them will be ready to take his place.

There are other areas of tension as well, though. The monk in the infirmary is becoming a burden possibly beyond the powers of the infirmarian to carry alone. Getting up every few hours at night and carrying a full work load during the day is coming to be too much. The prospect of the invalid having to go elsewhere, however, is something the community cannot bring itself to face and will probably never face. The infirmarian at moments finds this almost too heavy to bear and finds it difficult not to be short with others while carrying this burden. Awareness of this issue shadows the novitiate as well, as the sick man is much loved. Asking for someone to come in and help presents too many difficulties, financial and otherwise. The burden is very real and is one many people will recognize.

What is the lesson of this community for our present purposes? Once again, as with the Shalom community, the experience seems very positive. Once again, however, this "positiveness" is not about having many material resources. Materially, this group is very poor, almost destitute. Humanly, there are many shortcomings. Nonetheless, the riches of this group—as with Shalom—are its members. The older men have struggled through years of tribulation and questioning and have come to their own peace. They are honest in their dealing with one another without many major confrontations. They have lived together too long and know each other too well for that. (The story from the Desert Fathers that concludes this section could well be told of them.) They continue to work constructively for the good of their own house—a privilege of which our culture deprives many of the elderly, to their own loss and that of their juniors. Perhaps that is one of the major lessons of this house—the importance of what the old can give the young when they live in a context where their wisdom and experience as well as their present ability to work are valued. These old monks are not angels. There can be anger, conflict, and strain. But the years have taught them how to deal with these and the basic atmosphere of the house remains largely peaceful.

Perhaps another thing this community tells us is that the famous generation gap can be relativized in many cases. In my own community, I have heard more than one novice remark that the real test of the life, for her, is the older religious she meets. Perhaps the "generation gap" is more between groups of fifteen or twenty years' age difference rather than between the young and the very old. The attitude of much of our culture to old age may be causing us to squander one of our greatest treasures.

A story from the desert, whose source I have not been able to locate, provides a good example—though I am sure its tenor will horrify some. Two old monks decided that, having lived together for years, they should try to have an argument like the rest of humankind. One asked the other how to do it and he replied: "I will put something out on the floor and say 'It's mine' and then you say, 'No, it's mine.' And then we'll argue about it."

"All right," answered the first monk.

The other did as was planned and said, "It's mine."

"All right. Have it," said the first. And that was the end of their quarrel.

The above case needs to be complemented by another—almost its opposite but equally meaningful. A group of middle-aged and younger nuns in the Northwest found themselves in charge of their community's retirement center. Nursing care was supplied, in large part, by professionals, but this group of religious worked with the older sisters partly in nursing, partly for spiritual or pastoral care, and two worked outside in other apostolates. They lived in the same house and community as the old sisters and with time were puzzled at the awareness that they were increasingly feeling depressed.

It took a long time for them to realize what was happening. They were giving all day—either in a physical kind of service or with the moral effort involved in reading to, cheering up, or otherwise helping their older sisters. They reached the end of the day drained. Some of them began to experience the need to live elsewhere, but their order had no other house in the area and rental fees seemed high.

Finally, they began increasingly to share their experience with one another—when fatigue and business did not make this impossible. And a decision began to be born to form a separate community in the very heart of the present one. There was a section of the house little used at present where it could be possible to have a separate community room and kitchen, and sleeping space all around. The question was broached with some of those in the house, however, and the reaction was strong. The old nuns would feel abandoned, neglected, and rejected. What could possibly be the value of a segregation by age? The project was divisive, the establishment of a clique in the heart of the house. What could possibly be Christian about that? And so it went.

The prospective small community listened and reflected, experiencing some of what was said as truly quite damning. But the more they lived their present situation, the more they felt that continuing as they were doing was damaging. Finally, they went and spoke to the authorities in their order and obtained the permission to begin as a separate small community within the large one, on a trial basis.

All of this was six years ago. The community continues, though there have been one or two changes of membership. The group is happy together and blesses the day they made the decision. They find the fact of having support from people their own age truly a blessing and now feel they return from a hard day's work—and sometimes from keeping difficult hours—to a situation that truly gives life, support, and rest.

They have chosen to have a superior for their little group, though they know that many small communities have made a different choice. For themselves, they experience this decision as a source of peace. The superior is not the preconciliar kind of decision maker and ruler; all major decisions are discussed in community and made together. But she brings a certain clarity and preciseness to decisions made; her presence facilitates organizational issues; and, on occasion, she has a casting vote and has used it for the good of all. The group would not wish to change this option and yet feels as free as many who have chosen differently. They have experienced the last years as entirely positive and are grateful to have moved as they did. The older community now accepts their life-style and the harmony of the whole situation has improved.

This case needs to be set over against the previous one, since it seems, in so many ways, its opposite. In the first case, all age groups remain together; in the second, they felt the need to separate. In the first, contact with the elderly was seen as a source of life and wisdom; in the second it was a work from which rest was needed. In the first there was a kind of acceptance of whatever Providence sent; in the second, an active decision to change things. What is to be made of this contrast?

One obvious difference is the size of the groups involved. The first community is small in its totality; the second involves a large-scale retirement center. Human contacts sometimes require smaller numbers, though this is not always the case.

Moreover, in the second case the work in the retirement home was, precisely, the work of the younger group. It was less their home than their ministry. The fact that this work was with sisters of their own congregation made the feeling rather more familial, but nonetheless their duties there were indeed their work, as was the case for the infirmarian in the earlier example. There is a difference between living with older people, however helpfully, and spending one's whole day working for them. Whether patients are older or younger, hospital care on whatever level is no sinecure. The essential point, then, is not about age but about health or sickness and work. Had the earlier community been entirely hospitalized one would have had a very different picture.

It seems to me, however, that the true difference is on a much deeper level. Although general rules are often unhelpful (including this one!), to say that a community should never be divided simply according to age seems to make sense, since any such division can seem discriminatory. But what our heads say may not give sufficient space to the heart and to feeling. In the second case those involved knew in their experience and lives that what they were living was too draining.

Many religious women of my acquaintance, from many very different religious orders and communities, do not experience what they live in community as life giving. But many of these same women feel obligated to live with the situation as given in order not to rock the boat. They ask what their alternatives would be: they could go and live in an apartment with one or two others, but, if they are older, this hardly seems community living and it is certainly an expense for which their order may not be prepared. Further, it is not the life they have chosen and which they meant to take, the bad with the good. Living alone seems even "worse" along the same continuum. Splitting a convent building up into two or three communities seems divisive, as it did at first in our case above. And sometimes they find it difficult to ask for the improvements that would make this possible.

I could go on at length. The point is that in the case discussed, these women experienced their difficulty, reflected on a possible solution—even one that went against the theories—and then moved, at least on a trial basis, in the direction that their instinct seemed to suggest. This took more courage than is immediately evident, but it bore rich fruit. The suggestion this case makes to all of us is that daring to experiment can be a source of new life when that experiment is the fruit of really discerning and listening to the inner voices that speak. And, on the contrary, remaining in a deadening situation for lack of this courage is far from the experience of suffering as transforming, with which it can often be confused. The men in the first example accepted a difficult situation in terms of poverty, cold, insecurity for the future, and hard work, and they did so with serenity because much in what they live gives further life. The women in the second example experienced their fatigue as not giving life and chose to find a situation more humanly nourishing. Two apparently opposite attitudes and choices both led to positive results. Formulas fail. Only the heart really guides—the heart and reflection based on real hearing.

In terms of our discussion, what do these two cases say? The shadow of the first community was the fact that it seemed to be dying. Neither materially nor humanly did it seem to have the resources to live. Yet, paradoxically, the serene acceptance of death—without giving up prematurely—led to the emergence of new life. There is real radiance in what these men live now.

The shadow in the second case was the awareness of fatigue, discouragement, and depression, and this is hard for some religious people to face. "It is good to work until one is tired for the Kingdom of God," one hears. It is good to work until one is tired for whatever one truly believes, but thinking one can do without rest—emotional as well as physical—is what Jung calls inflation. These women were able to accept their weakness and limitations—in other words, they were not inflated—and to act in a way that would realistically address their needs. The result was that they, too, were able to build something positive and beautiful—and, what is more, to improve the quality of their giving and work. For them, too, what they do comes out of what they are.

All these questions are not irrelevant to marriage and family situations. More than one couple has had to experiment with ways of living that would allow each the necessary solitude and space, as well as the necessary companionship and help, amid all their varied obligations. Some very creative and new patterns of living have had to be found in some cases, but where people have had the courage to experiment to find these, they have often been very happy with the results. Here, as with other forms of community living, creativity and courage and honesty are crucially important. No easy and universal pattern exists.

The paradox, then, is that there is not one external way. People can make opposite choices and be right. The "way" is in our hearts and in the inner guidance that comes from openness to reality and truth, notably our own, and what these say. For deeper than the reality and truth around and in us is another Reality and Truth that speaks through these.

· 7 ·

BED AND BREAKFAST,
OR LARGE COMMUNITY?

"**I** was alone at Christmas and again at Easter. Thanksgiving, too, but we celebrated early to be together for that." Such statements are so frequently heard from religious in smaller houses today that they hardly need quoting. If one heard such a thing from a married woman one would think her hard done by. But religious are, it seems, meant to be made of sterner stuff. Or perhaps, not having chosen the married life and a family, they should take solitude for granted, some feel. But the fact is that such remarks about being alone often come from middle-aged and older people who remember when things were not thus, and they either grieve—or try to deny their grief.

In a wholly contemplative context, or one where the value of solitude is strongly stressed, such a situation might be valued by the one living it, as it is valued by someone very independent or introverted. But the phenomenon occurs also in the active communities that have modified their cloistered way of life so that they may be more present to those in need of their ministry. But in this case, those in need are at home—and the other religious, more often than not, with their families. Families, of course, have their needs as well. But when a young woman leaves her family to enter a religious community a good case could be made that she has thereby chosen to make her community her first family. What, then, is the meaning of this aspect of community life?

Today, there is a reaction against the strict and sometimes cruel way that separation from families was practiced in the past, at least among those old enough to have experienced it. Among the younger, there has often been no experience of the kind of separation their elders knew, and so there is the feeling that they should be as free to return home as if they were living in an apartment with a roommate. In that case, however, would they leave their roommate alone at the apartment? One wonders. And there are also questions one could ask about the notion of a community as a "hearth," a center of some sort of life—spiritual or communal.

So the question seems to be about the meaning of community. Have members any obligation to each other at all, or are all their obligations outside? Is contemporary religious life, notably active, a wholly individualistic situation where one can, in fact, do just about anything one wishes within the limits drawn by major lines of obedience? In other words, if I do my assigned job, is my daily life wholly my concern? Often it would seem so. Many speak today of bed-and-breakfast communities—places where people sleep and pick up what meals they need but into which they put a minimum of personal energy or caring.

As always, there is another side to this coin. Such people may also be receiving nothing from the community. They may have been assigned to—or even have chosen—this house because of its proximity to work or because it was the only one available for one reason or another, and there may be no one at all in the house with whom they have anything in common, whether by age, training, interests, or personality. What can they hope to build of community under such circumstances?

The traditional answer is that all these people do have something in common—their vocation, their spirituality. But what exactly does this mean? That they all want to serve the poor, minister to the sick, or teach? No, will be the answer; it is deeper than that. They are seeking to be like Christ: poor, servant of others, healer, or teacher. They can learn from each other how to live this more deeply.

This sounds good. After all, religious life is in some way meant to be a living of the Gospels. And one can always learn from others what their insights into such living might be. But the fact is that to touch these questions is to play with fire. To be willing to sit down with a group of others and see together what it might

mean to live certain parts of the Gospels is to risk one's life in
that context. It is to share one's weakness, one's darkness and
ignorance, one's fragility and struggles, one's desires to live more
deeply, and also one's cowardice, compromises, and lack of generosity. This takes much time, much trust, and much awareness
of being accepted. It is not possible to live in this way together
and yet keep whole spheres of one's life apart from such common
examination. This is a very risky situation. In the old days, when
most communities had a superior, one could at least hope that
the latter could keep such a risk from going too far for some
threatened individual. In a group without a designated authority,
one has not even this safeguard, and, as a result, some may fear
to touch any risky terrain at all. Many religious, notably active,
will say their commitment does not include this kind of dangerous
sharing. And one can certainly see why not. It is a situation
of total gift in a context one has not personally chosen and
with people one has not chosen and who may not, realistically
speaking, be sufficiently caring and careful. It is not difficult to
guess why most prefer to move toward self-giving more on their
own terms.

But where there is no sharing, is there community? In a marriage two people choose each other and try to set up a life and
family together. It may become very hard. They may come to
regret their choice or even separate. But while they are together
they can hardly avoid "putting something into the pot" of the
marriage. What they put in may be conflict and may lead to divorce. But, as Guggenbühl said, there is no escape from the other.

In active religious life, there is plenty of escape. This is not
necessarily reprehensible, considering both the risks of sharing
and the fact that some active vocations seem to be more about
doing than about being. But ultimately we do out of what we
are. Are such people choosing to have the "food" for their being
come out of work and external relationships rather than community? This may well be, and it is not necessarily undesirable.
But what, then, is meant by speaking of community as an essential
part of the religious life? Why would not living alone in an apartment be better? Or choosing a compatible roommate? Then,
at least, some sharing and exchange might become possible without becoming so threatening, and the human personality needs
this "food."

The issue is difficult. One solution that has been used successfully with groups of older religious might be adapted to other groups. Some large houses that used to be communities of pre-Vatican-II style have now become large communities of a slightly different style. Fifty, sixty, or seventy religious can live in a very large house—each with his or her own room and, usually, furniture, probably including a television or stereo and/or other forms of relaxation. Meals may be taken in a common dining room but need not always be. People come together when they wish and with whom they wish, and need not if they do not wish. Common business is settled at an occasional meeting but a co-ordinator can handle much of it. Such communities can absorb even people with psychological or other difficulties without too many problems because essentially people live alone there or by meeting with small groups of friends. It is like a small village.

It is easy to reflect that the postconciliar trend was to move away from such large communities toward small ones, so that people could come to know each other better and learn to relate more deeply. But the question is: Can one really relate deeply with just any group to which one is sent, by authority or by circumstances? Many hoped that this was the case. In a cloistered situation one is almost forced to do so—even without words—but as cloistered religious know, this can be purgatorial, even in a group that chooses and screens and votes on the acceptance of new members. In a noncloistered setting, when things are difficult or simply when the outer attractions are greater, what would make a person stay to struggle? Conviction of the value of the struggle might, but one would have to be willing to give considerable time to the process. And others would have to share this conviction and this willingness to work. Perhaps a model allowing individual apartments in a larger building with some common rooms is another solution. Some communities have done this with considerable success, more often men's groups than women's.

Perhaps the conclusion to all this is that there are various possible life-styles that either are or could be open to religious. Large communities with individual rooms allowing much independence; apartment complexes with common areas; individuals living separately, but with regular meetings in the same area; small-group living; and the like. What is doubtless important is that there be clarity about which style one has chosen and what it requires. Glorifying life in small communities seems a bad way to go, for it is easy to be officially living in a small community and yet in fact to be doing nothing of the sort—and this not culpably, for the necessary elements to make it humanly possible may just not be there. (This seems far more commonplace than most people like to admit.) Some compatibility, some willingness to share, some sense of safety and trust, some readiness to give time, effort, and concern to the business of living together—not just to make a cozy self-regarding unit but to live in common a common purpose or spiritual ethos—seem the minimal requirements for such a situation to work. And these are far from being always present. Lucidity on what this means is important. Gritting one's teeth and trying to force something to work when the necessary elements are absent may seem to be a virtue only in a totally moralistic world view. If life together gives nothing of any real value to those living it, what is its purpose? A friend of mine once said, "We are told that community gives us strength for ministry, but, in fact, my ministry gives me strength to deal with the struggles of community." She is not alone in this view and the phenomenon needs reflection. It is clearly about the fact that work can be "easier" emotionally than community living, in that the challenge and difficulty of relationship is usually less intense.

Where are we to go with this knowledge? Perhaps first to the realization that community, relationship, or marriage is a fire, that one does not get into its reality with impunity, and that one needs to ask oneself whether this is what one really wants. If so, there is a price to be paid. And perhaps its "shadow" is spiritual or psychological hoarding, avarice, and defensiveness. These are hard to renounce. Vulnerability is painful.

In the years just after the council, another friend, then still in her time of religious formation remarked, "You are building a religious life that only the elite can live. I need structures, if only to fight against them." If, in these postconciliar years, religious life truly allows space only for a very mature religious who knows in depth what her life is about, what help has been given to people to reach this stage? If help and support are lacking, it is not difficult to guess what will result. This question is as serious now as when it was asked, for the old protections—such as they were—are gone.

The above reflections largely concern the active life. For contemplatives, as has been said, the situation is different. They cannot escape into external activity. They have to be in the house for more than bed and breakfast. But there are other ways of escaping than going outside. Silence can be an escape, as can refusal to share one's real thoughts, feelings, and experiences. Rigidity, or the unwillingness to allow others space to be who they are and to need what they need, is as individualistic as needing one's own apartment, car, and life. And in a superior, this attitude can destroy others, especially when it is held—as so often—in the name of some very high-sounding ideals.

Community can be very hard in a contemplative setting, where the balance between solitude and sharing must be found by each house and each individual. Some are doing this very beautifully and with great spiritual freedom. Others are not managing at all. The issues seem different from those above, but in essentials they are much the same. The question remains that of what each one is called to put into the common pot that is community—in terms of time, in terms of honest sharing, and in terms of risk. The only difference lies in the way all of this is lived out.

I would like to end this chapter with a story cited by Joan Chittister.[1]

Let me tell you an old story from one of the conferences of the Master. There was a Benedictine community to whom nobody came. As the monks grew old, they became more and more disheartened because they couldn't understand why their community was not attractive to other people. Now in the woods outside the monastery there lived an old rabbi. People came from all over to talk to him about the presence of Yahweh in creation. Years went by and finally the abbot himself went into the woods, leaving word with his monks, "I have gone out to speak to the rabbi." (It was of course considered humiliating that a Christian community had to go back to the synagogue to find out what was wrong with them.) When the abbot finally found the rabbi's hut in the woods, the rabbi welcomed him with open arms as if he had known that he was coming. They put their arms around each other and had a good cry. The abbot told the rabbi that his monks were good men but they spread no fire, and the community was dying. He asked the rabbi if he had any insight into the work of Yahweh in their lives. The rabbi replied, "I have the secret and I will tell you once. You may tell the monks and then none of you is ever to repeat it to one another." The abbot declared that if they could have the secret he was sure his monks would grow. So the rabbi looked at him long and hard and said, "The secret is that among you, in one of you is the Messiah!" The abbot went back to his community and told his monks the secret. And lo! as they began to search for the Messiah in one another they grew, they loved, they became very strong, very prophetic. And the old conference ends: "From that day on, the community saw Him in one another and flourished!"

PSYCHOLOGY AND CONTEMPLATIVE LIFE—ENEMIES?

Sister Eleanor, a Temporary Professed in a contemplative community, came for help both because she felt so severely stressed that she wondered whether she needed a residential program, and because she could not decide whether to make final profession. She loved her community and the life, and they wanted her to stay. But both rigid use of authority and a rigid ethos had led to a great deal of repression and fear. People did not express themselves openly and honestly; the psychological health of several in the community was suffering. A sense of being cramped seemed prevalent. Yet there was fear of opening to outside influences— notably psychological, lest a psychologist not understand this way of life. Still, if it would help Sister Eleanor, a few were willing to consult a professional.

One frequently hears the remark, notably among some of the stricter contemplative communities, that psychologists cannot understand contemplative life. This judgment expresses a fear that is both very justified and not justified at all.

The view is very justified in that, as Guggenbühl already pointed out in the second chapter, there are certainly psychologies that, when used as a basis of therapy, seem to deny any value to sacrifice and seem to suggest that one ought to seek, ultimately, what is most psychologically and humanly comfortable and gratifying. Nonetheless, there is a truth at the root of this position. As pain in the body indicates that all is not well, so emo-

84

tional discomfort can be the same kind of indication. But as curing the physical symptom rather than finding out what the pain really indicates can lead to a worsening rather than an improvement of health, so a superficial cure of emotional discomfort can leave its deep roots untouched.

I still remember a humanities seminar in the 1950s with an outstanding university professor who was discussing Aldous Huxley's *Brave New World.* Students were asked whether anything in the book shocked them, and, if so, what. Little had. The professor, himself in his fifties, commented that the notion of gratifying all desire immediately lest it increase was basically inhuman, that the greatest works of the human spirit had been born of the refusal to gratify all desire superficially and immediately. One thinks of the relation between Dante and Beatrice, for example. To this professor, the students of the 1950s were already closer to the Brave New World than his generation in that they found the notion of instant gratification palatable. And the culture has continued to move in this way: the desire for immediate removal of all symptomatic pain is part of this tendency.

Some would blame part of this movement on the kind of psychology Guggenbühl mentioned, though sociologists find many other causes as well. In such a context, of course, the ethos of the contemplative orders is totally counter-cultural and incomprehensible. Is it counter-psychological as well? And, if it is, what does this mean? Is it an indication that psychology is too much in its infancy to incorporate the spiritual wisdom—and ascesis—of the centuries? Or perhaps that the contemplative ethos flies in the face of the dictates of physical and psychological health—with results not difficult to imagine? Yet this is contradicted by the psychological acumen of so many early texts, of writers like Theresa of Avila and John of the Cross, as well as by the classical strong stress on self-knowledge as the very basis of the spiritual life.

To answer our questions, however, let us return to the issue of whether contemporary psychology can understand the contemplative life. First of all, psychology is no more a science with one viewpoint than is philosophy. Compare, for example, the views of Freud and Jung, of Gestalt and Bioenergetics—and these are much closer to each other than to, for example, a behavioral approach. So what does *psychology* (or *therapy*) mean here? There are only individual therapists—each with a personal understanding of his or her work and with a personal philosophy, psychology, ethos. To say that no single one of them could understand—not even those who are themselves religious or contemplatives—is surely rather extreme and generalized.

But it is here that one reaches the crux of the question and the fear behind it. Perhaps the latter could be expressed in a double question. Have not the religious—notably the contemplatives—who have gone into this field sold out or betrayed their own specificity as religious or contemplatives? In other words, are not the two irreconcileable? Moreover, does not this kind of study give therapists a power over the less initiated which can be subtly destructive of the values they hold dear?

Everyone has doubtless heard the claims of psychologists that therapy respects the orientation of each individual. This is true in that therapy works, or normally claims to, for the development of each person's deep self. But it is also true that people in therapy change. Otherwise, why have therapy? And who is to say before the change in what direction it will go? In other words, who knows, on beginning, where the deep self of the individual really tends? To prejudge would be to control the process in advance, where the whole point is that one's viewpoint before therapy led to difficulties. There is, then, an issue of surrender. But to what?

Every psychology and psychologist has an understanding of the nature and workings of the human psyche. Some of these preclude the supernatural. Others, for pragmatic purposes, exclude theoretical issues to concentrate on behavioral change. These may seem the "safest" for a case like the community above, but dealing only with behavior still implies certain presuppositions. Who decides what behaviors are desirable, and on what grounds? Is all "cure" for the better? The deeper question is: What surrender will have to be made? And, to return to a still earlier question, is it compatible with contemplative life?

At this point, my own positions need to be stated, as I can hardly answer for others. If I place myself in the Jungian perspective, for example, I would consider that the surrender required in a community like Sister Eleanor's is first the surrender, or giving up, of fear—fear of the truth, fear of openness, fear of facing one's own reactions, fear of shadow material, of reality, of being seen for what one is and thinks, and, finally, the un-acknowledged fear that one's contemplative ethos cannot hold up under psychological scrutiny. What the surrender is *to* is basically the truth of one's being and feelings and of the realities of human existence. Where these can be faced, one can eventually move toward openness to a Self greater than one's own who emerges more as one also becomes his or her truer self.

Does this process require renunciation of the contemplative ethos? One would think just the opposite—at least if one believes such an ethos has roots in existential reality rather than in fantasy. Once again, my presuppositions come into play. If the contemplative ethos is about seeking union with God, I wonder how this can differ much from the position suggested in the last paragraph. To this end, I do not believe that rigidity is a help—neither in contemplative doctrine nor in the use of authority—for is not rigidity usually born of fear? If rigidity is born of fear, is the fear in question not about the reality of human nature that is seen as something to be forced into a mold? Rules, regulations, and orders can be used for this purpose—as was long the case in active communities as well, and sometimes still is. But the difficulty is that external conformity does not change the heart. It can, in psychological terms, cause introjection of the standards and values taught, or of the people seen as representing them. The result could be a dialectic between these introjects and the individual's tendencies. But in a sufficiently rigid situation there is not meant to be dialectic but only introjection. The personal is meant to die. This is frequently denied, but the lesson is clear.

If the "way of life" some contemplatives think psychology will not understand is one of rigidity, fear, and rejection of the real, then indeed it is true to say that psychology, or psychologists, will not understand. Even communication skills cannot be taught in a framework fearing communication. If, on the other hand, faith in the meaning and validity of the contemplative life is sufficiently deep to believe that looking at one's own truth and reality, and that of others, cannot hinder but can only help growth in the truth of God, then psychology need not be a dangerous or harmful to a contemplative community. Rather, it can be a help.

But in the wrong hands, it may not be a help. And in no case will the "work" therapy requires be easy. Real work of this kind never is, for it challenges one deeply and requires looking at much one has hidden. It is meant to transform.

Transform into what? the anxious will ask again. The answer is: Into one's real self, into the unique individual each one of us is meant to be, called to be from his or her depths, into a free and autonomous person whose obedience is not subservience to the collective but is a free choice of God.

The case above was studied, as is the project of this book, in terms of the community more than of the individual. The community has a decision to make if the quandary of this young nun—and the strain of others—is to be solved. Obviously, she herself has a personal decision to deal with, and that, too, is an individuation issue. But the community needs to choose whether to risk becoming a community of free and honest individuals, with the risks this choice entails, or whether, instead, to maintain its life-style largely by power and force, however freely this life-style may once have been chosen.

The shadow in this chapter, then, is basically fear—or even doubt, an unconscious doubt concerning the validity and strength of one's ethos and hence the unwillingness to put it to the test. Until this issue has been faced one builds on sand and false foundations. And yet, some fear in some cases is appropriate. Ignorance is what puts one in danger here. In today's world, even contemplatives need to know some psychology—and this is as it should be, since much of the best early psychology came from contemplative sources.

What would happen if one dealt with this whole issue in a dream? For a dream appropriate to this chapter I shall take one that was dreamt by someone in a situation not dissimilar to that of Eleanor. The dreamer was on a narrow cliff above a beach, standing with her back against the rock. (She had long been reflecting on whether to leave the community where she had spent the last years, although she continued to believe in the spiritual ideal of the life, no matter how much she suffered.) As she watched the sea she saw what seemed to be a tidal wave out away from land and, as she continued to watch, it drew closer and closer and loomed large. As she continued to watch, a sea lion began to emerge out of the water. It came close to her and she saw that it was smiling and friendly. When she awoke from this very vivid dream, suddenly the path ahead was clear. She decided to terminate her indecision, leave the community, and seek a life leaving her more inner freedom to grow.

Her case was one with a specific conclusion toward which the dream was an actual help. One is not always given quite such specific guidance from unconscious processes. If we return to the case of Sister Eleanor's community, it is worth remembering Jung's remark that it is important to choose an emerging new opposite without rejecting the one already chosen. If Eleanor, unlike our dreamer, can choose health and her contemplative life and community as well, she may find a rich combination— if, truly, they can be combined. In no way are health and the contemplative life intrinsically contradictory, though the way some live the contemplative life is another question. In other words, Eleanor's question is whether the choice of the community is intrinsically a choice of ill health for her. The answer will depend on whether the community can itself choose both values— psychological health and contemplative life. In reality this can be and has been done. The question is whether they will do it. In dream terms the issue may be whether the group is willing to face darkness, the shadow—as in the dream presented above, the dreamer came to make friends with the sea animal. We can imagine one community choosing truth and the risks of looking at darkness, and another choosing "purity" and rigidity that makes the community sterile. The truly contemplative choice, however, would seem to be the one involving openness to truth, at least if one believes that God is Truth.

The problem discussed in this chapter is not limited to contemplatives, though enclosure can make it more acute. Active religious life can include inner and outer structures that cause just as much excessive stress and, ultimately, illness. The choices, then, are the same, and they are never easy. Each individual in a community, whatever his or her life-style, can be brought by suffering to reexamine some very fundamental choices, and this is true of marriages and other communities as well. To submit one's life and ethos to an external arbitration—notably psychological—can seem very frightening indeed, and some people can never bring themselves to do it. My own impression is that the ability to do so is in itself frequently a sign of health and hope. This "third eye," with its objectivity, may be just what is needed for greater health and truth and a new beginning on the way. To return to a saying of the ancient Greeks, "The unexamined life is not worth living." Readiness to face another's view of one's own truth can be the readiness to submit life to such examination.

THREAD-GATHERING: A
CONCLUDING WORD TO PART ONE

The preceding chapters have studied cases from various religious communities—old and young, masculine and feminine, contemplative and active, clerical and lay. The key issue of
each case has been more universal than the community from
which it came: the effects of power; the challenge of living with
anger in oneself and others; various forms of fear, including fear
of psychological truth. There have been questions about the dialectic between general principles and individual choice; reflections on the value—and struggles—found in aging; discussions
of the need for boundaries; questions around weakness and
courage. All these are the stuff of every human existence—in
religious communities and outside. Before drawing these themes
together into some conclusions about community living, let us
look at some other human communities—marriages, families, a
tribal situation—and see what other material they supply for our
reflection on community, including the shadow material we meet
there and the ways in which dealing with it helps the movement
toward individuation.

As far as religious community goes, our previous cases do begin
to suggest one relatively inescapable conclusion. It is important
for religious, as for others living together, to know whether what
they want is a roof over their heads or whether they really do
want community and relationship. If it is this latter that they
seek, it is equally important to know that relationship and community do not just grow by themselves. Time, attention, com-

mitment, mutual concern, effort, and willingness to work with difficulties as they arise are necessary. Without them the venture almost has to fail. This is an axiom in marriage counseling; why should it be different here?

When I was in early adolescence, I knew a man who was externally very successful but who in fact had much to suffer behind the scenes—notably in his marriage. Yet he remained courageous. One day he remarked to me: "Life is like a kind of coin-changing machine: you put a nickel in and get five pennies out. But the world is full of people who want their pennies without putting in a nickel." I think he told me the secret of his life—and I think the analogy holds.

Part Two

Other Forms of Community

·9·

EXCLUSION OR INCLUSION?

Another place where community may be studied is in the ways it manifests itself in a tribal structure. While such a subject would perhaps be best studied by use of scientific work on tribal societies as they are known and still exist in some places, I have chosen, as a basis for this chapter, not an anthropological but a fictional study of a tribe. There are various reasons for this choice, not the least of which is that fiction, in its place, can be even more universal than science, even easier to relate to experiences we all share. The author of the novel in question did, in fact, base her work on much study and research, but the human significance of the incident I want to discuss has to do with a more universal experience than that known only in what we usually consider tribal living.

The Mammoth Hunters, by Jean Auel, is part of a series called *Earth's Children.* The heroine, Ayla, is orphaned by an earthquake and finds shelter with a group called the Clan of the Cave Bear— a group less humanly advanced than that from which she was born. Later, cursed by and expelled from the Clan, she lives alone until she meets a man of her own kind, Jondalar, who had been wounded by a lion on his journey through her terrain. Together they move on to find the Mammoth Hunters, people more of their own kind. These latter are increasingly taken with Ayla and Jondalar and will soon be asking them to be adopted and stay.

Meanwhile, however, Jondalar warns Ayla not to speak of the

people who brought her up and whom these more developed tribes think not even human. She retorts that she owes her life to the Clan and will not keep such silence. The following incident results.

Ayla is a medicine woman and warns the quarreling husband and mother of a pregnant woman that their fighting can make her lose her baby.

> "What does she [Ayla] know about it!" Frebec [the husband] sneered. "Raised by a bunch of dirty animals, what can she know about medicine? Then she brings animals here. She's nothing but an animal herself. You're right, I'm not going to let Fralie [his wife] near this abomination. Who knows what evil spirits she has brought into this lodge? If Fralie loses the baby, it will be her fault! Her and her Mother-damned flatheads!"[1]

Ayla responds to this attack by running out into the cold and away from the group. Jondalar persuades her to wait for better weather to leave but she expresses determination to return to the cave where she lived alone. Jondalar reminds her of the loving welcome received from all the others, but all Ayla can see is the hate of this one man, Frebec. When friends in the camp speak of what they could do to make her happier, she responds, "I think Frebec not like to have *animal* so close." Reminded that Frebec is only one person she responds, "But Frebec is Mamutoi [the name of the tribe], I am not."[2] It is this reflection, heard by others, which prompts the tribe to move to offer her formal adoption.

This dynamic is something that will be familiar to anyone with even the experience of groups we find in grammar school: the sense of exclusion when even one person expresses hate and contempt; the way belonging to a despised group—even when one values them oneself—can make one feel excluded; the extraordinary ability of the human person to identify himself or herself as the despised person or thing—like Ayla calling herself an animal—even when that identification is false but fits another's mentality. All these are processes one finds even in a group of schoolchildren. They reflect the human condition and are reminiscent of the rather terrible pages of Jean-Paul Sartre on what the "glance" of the other does to one just by looking in a way one presupposes to be unfriendly.

The crux of the question is, of course, where the locus of one's self-appreciation and self-judgment lies. Security in oneself makes others' negative judgments matter less. Of course, much will depend on that other's personal value to me and how much I care about his or her judgment. Much will depend, too, on the type of personality one has—introverted or extraverted, concerned or not about community living, concerned or not about *this* community's ethos.

The schoolchild who is made a scapegoat—whether because of personal idiocyncracies or because of prejudice against a group—can bear the marks for life. If the prejudice is against some group of which he or she feels proud—a religion, perhaps, or some political group—then a kind of "martyr for the truth" mentality can prevent much of the damage. It is the others who are wrong and the martyr who is right. But when the issue is one of weakness, smallness, ugliness, or other targets of prejudice, a child can carry the negative self-judgment for years into adulthood, more so if the child is sensitive and has no counter-balancing experience.

What has this to do with community? Much indeed. Sensitivity to slights and negative reactions from others is a factor that can make community living very difficult. When the sensitivity is unrealistic, it has to do with inner material one projects. In this case there will be hurts no matter what happens externally. Where there has really been a negative interaction, sometimes an honest assertive response can clarify it. Sensitivity here can be called realistic, and interaction of this style can build relationship. But sometimes the hurt simply has to remain, as a part of human living. One must hope that it is not one's own inner issues that are leading one to magnify either slights or the importance of the person slighting, for thus life in community becomes difficult all the time. One often hears, for example, "When So-and-so is out of the house, office, meeting, I function much better, I feel so much freer and happier." This feeling can be very real. But one can legitimately ask oneself what gives So-and-so that much power, or why one gives it oneself.

In the excerpt above, Ayla has been warmly received by everyone in the community except this single person. True, she is aware of the prejudice against the Clan where she grew up. She has heard the insults "animals," "not human," and "flatheads" before, and this has hurt or angered her. She has not, however, been called by these names herself, especially in this way. Her background in the Clan, however, where she was also not wholly accepted since her appearance showed her clearly to be one of the Others, gave her a history of nonacceptance, pain, and insecurity, into which this new experience played. Now, this one rejection is sufficient to make her remember all the past hurt, reenter past rejection, and want to leave her new home and return to the relative security of solitude—though she truly minded the solitude. But at least when one is alone there is no one around to hurt one.

This novel illustrates well the fragility of the excluded—whether the exclusion is real or simply an interior pattern built up over the years. What is important in this question is that if personal self-acceptance and comfort with oneself are insufficient, it is difficult to be happy living in community. Lacking these strengths, inner self-rejection can be projected out onto whoever seemingly or really is rejecting. It is clear that people with much inner security and balance can find themselves living with others who do not accept them and who can be insulting or hurting in their contacts, and of course this will hurt. The decision that living in the same group with someone else is undesirable can be necessary for people of many different kinds, not only the insecure. But for those already living an inner "self-exclusion," even a community that could be all right is not. And that is important to know. For in this case there is a level and kind of pain quite different from that involved in a calm objective understanding that one is not meant to live with certain kinds of people or certain individuals.

In other words, in any group there is likely to be a person or two who is nonaccepting of some other, and that nonacceptance is always likely to be painful. The question is: If one's other relationships in the group are friendly and happy; if there is sufficient gratifying experience in the other areas of one's life, does this single question really need to cloud the whole of life in that place? The question is worth examining. If one cannot breathe freely or be oneself when X is in the room, is it because X is so important, or because one is very sensitive and needs others—or why? Perhaps one needs to wonder whether the issue is one of dreaming of an earthly paradise where life will be cloudlessly happy, as in the maternal womb. For, if the question is put this way, perhaps the unreality of certain expectations can come clear.

This said, however, it is also important not to go to the other extreme. Perhaps there is no earthly paradise without mosquitos and spiders; perhaps it is impossible to return to a womb where all is uniformly helpful, warm, and peaceful. (Though, increasingly, experiments are suggesting that even intrauterine experience is not always thus!) But it is also not necessary to conclude that life in community needs to be a constant purgatory. And if it is that, whatever the reason, why not take the needed steps to change this situation? One meets people willing to living in a situation that is in no way life giving for them and who will respond to questions on the subject, "Oh, well, that is life." In no way are the above reflections meant to encourage such an attitude. If the experience of living in community does not contribute something positive—indeed, much that is positive—to one's life and experience, why would one continue to live in this way? To say that one is vowed to this marriage or this family or this community is an insufficient answer. A vow is traditionally a promise of something better. If life in this community is not better than life without it, one needs to reflect seriously on what is going wrong.

One final issue is the importance of such experiences for positive growth in self-knowledge. If snubbing "hooks" something in me, learning to deal with the "hook" may make the snubs far less important, and it will certainly reveal things to me about myself if I can identify the hook. So once again, paradoxically, much of the "work" one has to do to live constructively in community, whether by changing or by staying, is interior to oneself.

Saying this, however, is treading a very fine line. One hears constantly remarks like, "X drives me crazy and is very rude at all meetings, but I just put it out of my mind." This solution is *not* what is being advocated here. Putting a problem out of one's mind, or repressing it, allows the issue to build up within—unseen, more often than not. It is a very different conclusion to say that one will work with the inner issues aroused by this disagreeableness until finally its manifestations come to matter less or to be understood. They will still be felt and noticed, by some more than others. But at least at times the reaction passes, or if it does not, one knows why. Repressed reactions, on the other hand, do not pass but come out later—in other forms and perhaps with other people. Sometimes a real hatred for one person develops, not because the person deserves all that hate but because he or she comes to be the repository of years of hidden anger. Much needs to be unblocked before the hate can be dispelled.

But there is another issue closely connected with that of tribal structure, as well as that of many other communities, and that is the question of a tribal or collective ethos. This subject has already been discussed above in related connections but some other aspects emerge here.

The tribe, the collectivity, has its own unwritten codes, its own collective judgments and ways of thinking, and one finds these equally strongly in unstructured groups. The pressure on individuals within this collectivity to conform is strong in proportion to the degree of unconsciousness involved, though there can also be very conscious and free decisions to conform. Tribal taboos can be an expression of such collective thinking. In what we call a primitive mentality one could hardly conceive that the gods would not punish an infringement of what the tribe thinks wrong. With growth in consciousness comes the awareness of the source of some taboos, and this can lead to their relativization. It may be taboo in my culture to steal, but if I reflect that the purpose of this taboo (in the loose sense of the word) may be to protect people's rights to their own property, then, if I am starving, I may feel that taking what I need to live may not, after all, be immoral. If, however, my mentality is still literally and unconsciously that of the taboo, then no matter what my state of poverty I will fear to steal. If I am religious, I will think God will punish me. In any case, I will feel I have done wrong, if I am thinking collectively. I will feel less like a full and good member of the group if I steal.

This may seem like an issue of individual conscience, and so it is. But it is also an issue of community formation of conscience. Any community—tribe, campus, religious group, family—has a certain unspoken collective ethos. The more numinosity is connected to the community, the stronger the hold of that ethos. Infringement—even internally—can lead to a sense of exclusion. But if growth in human maturity is about becoming individuated, the process naturally leads to emergence from the collective ethos.

One may choose again some of the same values. Our collective ethos may forbid murder, and the individuated person may make the same choice. But the decision is coming from a different and freer place in the psyche. Exclusion or inclusion in the whole no longer have the same kind of value. This is not to say that the collectives in question are not valuable—nor that they are not valued. But the valuing is freer. Once again, the judgments of others may no longer have quite the same kind of hold. And the fear of making free and different decisions can decrease. Such people can be frightening to the collectivity, of course. As such, they may find themselves actually excluded as threats. But this is less the case, one hopes, in more "conscious" groups. At any rate, such groups may be more pluralistic.

What is the fruit of this chapter's reflection? Some possible sources and experiences of extreme vulnerability to a single person or group have been examined. The importance of working with the issues involved and trying to grow in lucidity about them and oneself—if one is to live in community peacefully—has been stressed. The mirage of thinking any community will be the "earthly paradise"—or the maternal womb—has been exposed. And finally the interrelationships between growth in individuation, or personal development, and awareness of the collective mentality have been discussed. All these factors are important to successful community living.

Part of the shadow material here involves personal sensitivity. Part also involves the power one can give another and his or her rejection. Part involves the tendency to personal self-rejection into which another's rejection can play. Finally there is the essential issue of having one's center of judgment in the collective ethos rather than in oneself. The whole journey of individuation is about moving beyond this point—even when, later on, one freely chooses some of the same values as one's own. When this occurs, these values themselves are part of one's own life, choice, and values, in an individual, personal, and now really free way. What is externally the same becomes very different because of the being of the person choosing and the freedom of that individual being. From outside one cannot often know from which place another's choices are coming. Once again, the sources of one's deep action are part of the secret center of one's own heart, the place where real freedom is born.

· 10 ·

A THERAPEUTIC COMMUNITY

The community described by Jacqui Lee Schiff in her book *All My Children*[1] is extraordinary in many ways. For one thing, it considers itself a family, rather than a community, though it is composed more of adults than of children. For another thing, this "family" is basically therapeutic.

This author and her husband were both social workers, and were distressed over the fate of schizophrenics considered to be incurable. Both worked as therapists. A turning point in their lives occurred when a young man whom Jacqui was treating in her home gave every sign of becoming dangerous. She called her husband, Moe, to return home from work, and when both therapists tried to deal with Dennis's terror and hate, this six-foot university student was asked by Moe, "What is it you want, son?" "Without another word . . . [Dennis] assumed a fetal position, cuddled into my [Jacqui's] lap, and attempted to nurse."[2]

This wordless reaction opened both therapists to an increasing awareness of the need of many young schizophrenics to experience "reparenting"—to relive with loving parents what had been lived badly in their first experience of being parented. They began to call each young person who came to live with them their "baby" and to allow each to regress to a situation like the one above and grow from there. The results were outstanding cures for more than one, but this usually involved a definitive departure from the family of origin to become part of this new therapeutic family.

For our present purposes, one important aspect of this situation

102

was that, despite the fact that it was Jacqui and Moe who were the therapists, much of the necessary interaction for each "child" occurred in the whole group—the "family," or community. It was there that people worked through problems; it was the group that went seeking someone who tried to flee without really wishing it; it was, ultimately, largely the group that healed. "Obviously a therapy group," one might say. Yes, and yet this was a "family" or community living together all the time.

If you walk into our big living room in the late afternoon or early evening when most of the children are at home, it might, at a quick glance, seem like many another comfortable, middle-class home—except that the family is larger. At the moment we have twenty children. There are no locks on the doors, no white-coated attendants. We are a family. A carefully structured family. And if you look and listen for a few minutes, the structure becomes apparent.

If a child misbehaves, he is never banished to his room or in any way isolated, since isolation is the very last thing a withdrawn schizophrenic needs. He may be spanked or made to stand in a corner in the living room where we all sit. The heavy wooden restraining chair we constructed with auto safety belts is not used for punishment, but to enable us to control episodes of pathological violence without separating the upset youngster from the activities of family life.

There is laughter in our house. But there are no private jokes among the children or the parents. And before Moe and I even say something teasing, we identify it as teasing. For we have learned that our children incorporate every word we utter in a concrete, literal way. Everything we say or do has an exaggerated importance to them because they depend on us to teach the things that will create in them a healthy, functional attitude toward life— things they missed in their first childhood.[3]

What are the bases of this truly extraordinary family/community, and how does it work? Moe and Jacqui found at their first meeting that,

. . . from entirely different backgrounds, living on opposite sides of the continent, we had each independently been developing our lives along the same lines. We thought the same way, and we felt the same way about nearly everything from politics to child care.[4]

The basis for this family, then, was a couple who already had much in common as individuals, and who met with a certain level of maturity already established. The regression incident that opened this chapter served as a lesson for them, in that they learned from each "child's" awareness of his or her needs what the truly therapeutic approach for them was to be. They learned step by step, requiring of the "children" increasing cleanliness with time, as one would with any baby; exercising authority in the way one does with a not-yet-rational infant. But also, their care and concern for these "children's" health touched the latter deeply. For some it was a first experience of such care. And each "child" progressed from early regression to gradual return of maturity, some to outstanding health and therapeutic service in their turn.

Of Scandinavian background, Jacqui became Jewish when she married Moe, and their household "is a Jewish household, an expectation which we communicate to all our children. In all areas of ethical and moral behavior we try to present a clear, consistent image and an even balance of authority and understanding. . . ."[5] These "children" need to know clearly what is the mother's role and what the father's. They need to be told that they are valued, seen as beautiful and good, despite their faults and the necessary corrections, for these positive images are what was lacking in their first experience. Clear positive demands and expectations are important here, as they are for any small child, and Jacqui's experience with Transactional Analysis is a factor in her conviction that each one needs to feel "OK" in himself or herself.

This all sounds lovely, but the reality was hard. Some of the "children" were dangerous, and Jacqui formed the habit of reviewing which ones were upset with her before going to sleep— a half-watchful sleep—at night. Others would "act out" as a way to control her, even in self-damaging ways, like throwing themselves downstairs. Some turned out to be incurable. And harder still, if the "children" felt the parents gave up on one "child," this became a threat to all the others. "Will they give up on me, too, then?" was a recurring question—and one asked with reason, given the behavior of almost all. Thus, much in the "children's" behavior was, in one way or another, an attempt to control the parents and their own fate. At every moment, decisions had to be made of what to allow, what to control or punish, and what absolutely to forbid. With time, Jacqui and Moe learned often to trust the child's own instinct as to what was needed, even if this meant breaking radically with rather universally accepted principles of therapy. They learned, too, to trust their own instincts more. But nonetheless, the needs of training, discipline, and mutual protection had also to be met—and that in very difficult circumstances. In some cases, the real need was to be spanked by both parents, when leniency could be understood as another kind of lack of love. The "children" themselves spoke of their need for authority.

So far what has been discussed has concerned mostly Jacqui and Moe. But, again, the whole community was involved—including the couple's "natural" "normal" children. When someone ran away, or was suicidal or in need of supervision, everyone helped. The health of each was a common responsibility, though the "parents" carried the weight. Everyone worked together, and all together shared their weakness and pain. The one thing for which people really could be sent away was not wanting to work for improvement or to try to get well.

One essential lesson for some of these "children" was "not to discount." Some—and these not all from poor families—hardly felt heat, cold, or hunger because they had been taught to pay no attention to their feelings or needs. Jacqui remarks, "One of the reasons our children get well . . . [is] that we try not to discount. We consider all behavior purposive and try always to confront it in some way."[6] Discounting always plays a part in the development of schizophrenia, she remarks. Another essential factor in the cure, especially for some, was to learn no longer to split the Bad Child from the Good Child (to use terms from Transactional Analysis). When they could see both the bad and the good within themselves, they were on the road toward health, and the common uncomfortable experience of the gray area in so much of our lives. Finally, Jacqui remarked in the latter part of her book, her silent withdrawal before passive-aggressive behavior—a withdrawal she hardly realized—was in fact meeting passive aggressivity with more of the same. It was important here, too, to learn to confront. And yet, at the same time, it was important for each child to learn that it was not only when he or she was intelligent or functional that he or she would find love. If it is all right to be a spontaneous child at first, one eventually learns to be an adult who can also be in touch with the inner child. Without that, life can become very sterile, and hardly healthy.

It is easy to think that all this is a very specialized experience and has nothing to say to the rest of humanity about family and community life. But to believe this is to be unaware of the amount of pathology in each of us—sometimes deeper the more it is controlled and hidden from view. A psychiatrist friend of mine once remarked that working with the seriously disturbed is most enlightening as it shows us what we all, to a lesser degree, do and feel. So it is worth reflecting on the Schiffs' experience to see what it might say of community in general.

First, there is the issue of seeing one's community as a family. How far does such a comparison hold for adult communities? Clearly, in a family—particularly with young children—there are authority figures not found in the normal adult community. One of the risks in some forms of religious community, among others, has been allowing someone to take a parental position, to the detriment of the adulthood of other members. One also hears the remark that religious, and some other, communities are not families because members are not bound by the familial kind of love and blood relationships. I think the Schiffs' story says something about the ability of love to create a family in very unlikely cases.

Is this an appropriate model for most communities, however? I believe not, in the sense that the finality is different. A family is born around the love of two people and it nurtures the young until they are old enough to live on their own. A community is normally a group of adults living together for a common reason— not in the kind of love that unites husband and wife and not, again, normally, for the nurturance and education of the young, though communities also have to train their young. So communities are not families. However, families are to some extent communities—notably as children grow older. And there are common factors in both, some of which the experience we are discussing illustrates.

One such factor for reflection is the need the Schiffs experienced to withdraw their "children" from their previous families. Obviously, one can retort—the previous families helped to cause their illness. This is certainly not true of the families from which most people come to a marriage or a community.

Valid as this objection may be, it is a fact that the "children" we are discussing had to leave their old life to embark on the new. How many marriages have been vitiated by a wife's tendency to "return home to mother" every time the going gets rough, or by a husband's inability to get out from under his dependence on mother or father, whether this dependence is exterior or interior? In religious communities, cloister used to supply a total—and sometimes brutal—separation from families. Perhaps in reaction, one can now find situations in which one wonders which is the prime community or choice of life of a given religious, as we saw in chapter 7. One does have to make choices, and growing up involves a choice in this regard. One takes on new obligations and a new life, and if one's real energy and commitment are not there, this weakens the whole fabric of community living.

Another interesting point is the therapeutic activity of the whole group. This can be a sore subject in both families and religious communities at present, but it needs to be examined. "We are not a therapeutic community (family)," one hears people say. "If someone has problems they need to be worked out elsewhere, with a counselor or someone. I don't believe in 'letting it all hang out.' I need my privacy. And I don't need to come home from the fatigue of a working day into what amounts to a group-therapy situation." One can understand this point of view, notably since it is a fact that people often end a day's work tired, drained, and needing relaxation for their own survival. And, in a contemplative community situation, time is often short and people live together all their lives. Thus privacy is exceptionally important here.

On the other hand, one can get some clue into part of the real issue if one looks at an alcoholic family, that is, a family where someone is an alcoholic. In such a group, everyone is involved. Certain typical behavior patterns emerge in all the other members of the family, and it is all in response to this one phenomenon. For the family to refuse to deal with the issue implies not only that the alcoholic member does not get the needed help but also that all the others continue in patterns that are not healthy. This can be extraordinarily damaging to all. No one wants the repeated scenes, confrontations, denials, tension, and strain of facing someone with this issue. But that is the price of health—for each one and for the group. And there are other addictions—smoking, overeating, and overworking (too rarely seen in its potential for damaging relationships), not to speak of drug abuse. Some of these may be less damaging to others and the group but they also cause their reverberations within the whole. Each person needs the privacy to live in peace and not be challenged on every little thing. But also, "No man is an island." If one's reactions to things that are distressing in others are patterned on the turtle or ostrich, then it is time to do some looking at one's own pathology, though that is equally true if there is a need to haul absolutely everything out onto the carpet. It is important to know not only how one feels but why one shares or decides not to share feelings in a given situation. And this is an issue that has to do not only with one's own psyche but with personal impact on the entire living situation or group.

Does all of this constitute "a therapeutic community"? Not in the sense of our present chapter. But any group that is appropriately honest is therapeutic to some extent. (There has been more than one reflection on the common roots of the German words for "wholeness," "health," and "salvation.") Peace is an important value, but is avoiding all openness about one's feelings the way to any real peace? More than one friendship has been deepened by the honest sharing of conflicts and doubts. On the other hand, some relationships have been destroyed that way. As in the chapter on "Bed and Breakfast," the basic question is, What kind of community is intended here? A common habitation only? Or a group that shares life? This latter requires far more risk. But some who live it find it well worth the effort.

Jacqui speaks of the importance of structure. This, too, is an important contemporary issue. "We have no structure," one often hears. But that, too, is obviously a kind of structure, and especially when it is based on a principle that one never wants to have any structure. The basic point involved seems to be that any structure at all might impinge on someone's freedom. But if someone wants absolute freedom, why live with others at all? Solitude might be a more appropriate choice. The important question here is clarity about the reasons for living together and the style desired for this life together. As was said above, some groups apparently living in community would be happier and more in line with what people wanted if each one lived alone and there were some common rooms in which to meet others when one wished—a situation one finds in many retirement homes and that some religious communities are beginning to set up. Other communities include some people who wish the above style and others who really wish for much more common activity and sharing, which can mean that both are hampered in what they seek. And the same is true of families, but the difficulty there is that almost each year of a child's growth after a certain age brings different needs. The gamut from no togetherness to excessive togetherness is wide, and each individual has different needs. It is also important to relate one's own needs to those of others—without being totally selfish, and without such self-sacrifice that one loses one's own identity, a risk that seems greater for women. It is all about learning who one really is. But when the word *structure* rouses inner fear, resistance, even panic, it is worth some reflection to find the real reason why.

Jacqui next speaks of the things she and Moe had in common, even before they met. At the risk of belaboring the obvious, this point needs more reflection. Both in communities and in marriages, when people have little to share, living together can be very painful. One person wants jazz playing all day, another wants classical music, and another wants silence. One person thinks manners are very important and another finds them stuffy. One person comes from a very cultured background and another thinks anything above the comics insufferably "highbrow." One could continue this list forever. Exponents of Christian communities and some believers in romantic love in marriage have insisted that all this should not count: all that matters is love. And all that matters *is* love. But love is about sharing, as well as about mutual respect. If the dialogue and sharing between two or more people is really such that very much in their lives, even what they bring into the relationship, is common (which is not to say "similar" but is to say "shared" or "sharable"), it is amazing what can be built in terms of community. I have lived in situations where people of totally different backgrounds have been very happy together in real depth. But that has been where, even if the past had been very different for each, the orientation for present and future was truly common. This can be as important.

But much common living is needed to make this clear and live it out in truth.

The following passages speak of the need for clear expectations—for the "children" in our example, but for the community as well. Perhaps the same is true for any community. Playing everything by ear may lead to living nothing stably, ever.

The next issue is one that is already familiar—that of attempts to control others, whether by some form of acting out, by manipulation, or even by simple temper. Surely this is so universal as to need everyone's reflection. The problem in many marriages and communities is that many people are not trained to recognize attempts to control them, nor do they know how to deal with them. They experience a kind of dull resentment and anger and do not quite understand the source. Learning to bring such issues out into the open of one's consciousness is a first and very important step if one is ever to deal with the external issue. Believing that all anger and resentment are wrong, is, of course, the perfect way to make this process impossible and to arouse guilt feelings over what could have been one's greatest help toward clarity and enlightenment.

Nonetheless, the Schiffs learned to trust their "children's" own instincts as to what they needed, and this is perhaps the greatest lesson of all. If a schizophrenic with a totally negative prognosis knows what he or she needs to move toward health, it is surely very important for us to learn to trust one another and ourselves—and thus to respect one another and ourselves—as to what we really need. If a community or marriage is based on a truly respectful interaction on these subjects, it is hard to see how it could go deeply wrong. But this point is not easy to reach. The superficial version of it is a kind of laissez-faire where I really do not care much what you do. And that is not the point at all. It is important to learn to mind one's own business and live one's own life. But it is also important to be who one is with others. That is Guggenbühl's "painful confrontation," but, to him, it is an excellent way toward individuation.

It is precisely in this regard that Jacqui's remark about seeing all behavior as purposive, about not discounting, is important. "I have a headache, but it doesn't matter," "I'm exhausted, but it will pass," "I could murder everyone in the house, but a night's sleep will take care of it"—how many of these remarks are familiar to us all (not to speak of ulcers, digestion problems, rashes, sleep-lessness, and so many other signals of our bodies)? What do such signs say to us? Why do we not want to listen? All these questions need their own attention. And so when Jacqui says she learned not to meet passive-aggressive behavior with more of the same, this implies the importance of learning not to withdraw from conflict and from facing issues and questions, at least within, but at times externally as well. All this takes time and energy, which is to say that community and marriage take time and energy. They don't just happen. If one is not able or willing to make this expenditure, maybe the question of living together needs to be examined.

This therapeutic community, then, has many things to teach anyone living with others, and it raises many questions that all of us have to face. The Schiffs lived this in a specialized—and surely heroic—way. But life together always demands at least some minor kinds of heroism, for it both unselves us and helps the growth of the deep self—if, that is, one learns how to live it wisely. The Schiffs gave up what must surely have seemed a nor-mal, natural married and family life with their own children to open their hearts to this wider and far more demanding family. Perhaps, on the road to individuation, most of us have to open ourselves to what is, in Jung's term, "unnatural"[7]—whether this demand comes through others, through the unconscious, or through life itself and its pain. If one can grow to meet this de-mand of the other/Other then one comes to learn what it is to love. And surely that is what community is ultimately about.

· 11 ·

PRIORITIES

Sally and John R. have been married for twenty-five years—happily, it seems to those around them. But there is tension and strain. John is an executive vice-president of his company and works long hours. Sally is proud of his position that makes it possible to keep their three children in private school and college. But she feels John never has time for her. John, on the contrary, feels he is getting double messages. One is: "Continue, I am proud of you." The other is: "Why don't you drop it all and be attentive to me?" "I'm damned if I do and damned if I don't," he remarks. On the other hand, John loves athletics, notably cross-country skiing, and he wonders why, if she wants him to spend time with her, Sally is never willing to share such sports with him.[1]

At first sight, this situation looks simple. Surely, John can give Sally the assurance of a few hours a week, be it only a dinner date, or perhaps a nightly hour or two? Surely Sally can bestir herself to learn to share at least one sports activity with him? Needless to say, things don't work so easily. When John returns home from work, he is tired, spent, without energy. Watching the news is about all he feels able to do. He is not effervescent at dinner, even when the children are home, and energy does not really return until bedtime, when Sally has already long since gone to sleep. Weekends might be better, but he feels this is a good time for sports with his friends, and to do some work around the house and garden and be with the children. With Sally also, of course, but this rhythm hardly seems to meet her needs.

112

Would it be better if she learned to ski? Sally is not gifted at sports and has learned from painful experience that, when she tries to share such activities with her husband, not only is it scarcely enjoyable for her but also he must make heroic efforts to keep his patience. He is quickly bored and obviously would be happier sharing this activity with more athletic friends. One is forced to conclude that willpower—or goodwill—is not enough to solve these questions.

A second level of possible solution, and one that seems to have been suggested to the couple more than once, would recommend that both cultivate more independence. Cannot Sally live her own life more and need John less? Cannot John be content to share sports activities with others? The difficulty with this solution is obvious. Certainly each can live his or her own life. What, however, will become of their relationship in the process? Could they end up moving toward divorce because one is busy and the other can't ski? It sounds ridiculous, but many people know it is not.

Was the marriage a mistake? Did the two not have enough in common to embark on a common life? In college they seemed to share much—they came from similar backgrounds; had similar social expectations and similar levels of intelligence; they went to football games and plays and dances together happily. What happened?

I believe there is a basic question concerning life options that people find it difficult to articulate when embarking on a common venture like marriage or even some community situations. Yet without this articulation, much can go awry. What, for example, is each person's honest need for togetherness, and what is his or her equally honest need for space? As more than one marriage has gone on the rocks for lack of sufficient togetherness or relationship, so I have known more than one become impossible because at least one partner was not able to give the other sufficient space or allow the other to take it. It is difficult to know in one's twenties how such needs will evolve, but personality type and basic tendencies can certainly give a clue—if one can find them within the maze of the socializations so easily imposed on the young.

Again, how important are material things? If one person finds it truly important to live in upper-middle-class style and without serious financial worries, and the other thinks all such issues secondary, the result is as clear as it would be in the case of one being very concerned about manners and courtesy while the other grew up comfortable with rudeness or fighting. Small things cease to be small over the years.

More important still—and this is more a question for the individuals than for the relationship—are some personal priorities contradictory? Is Sally asking the impossible in wanting her financial and social situation as comfortable as it is and yet wanting a husband with much free time and little fatigue? Is John asking his wife to be something she simply is not? Realism is a key virtue in relationship.

But I think equally key is the question of common priorities. If a young couple can say to each other, "Money is necessary and much would be nice, but more important is the relationship, the family, common interests, and activities," then a certain apportionment of time results. Work time and energy will be kept within certain limits—barring untoward events or circumstances. Time will be spent cultivating common pursuits and sharing interests. Perhaps nonetheless the two will grow apart; this can happen as people change and mature. But it seems more likely that with work on the relationship, the family, communication and sharing, something of a living community, family, and marriage can be built. As Guggenbühl remarked, this may involve sharing difficult and painful things, but the very self-exposure to the other moves one toward individuation. It also deepens relationship.

It is difficult to see how this can happen at a lesser price. The idea that relationships can flourish without effort and attention is surely an illusion. Even friendships need some time and sharing to live, and friendships have not the day-to-day rubs that life together produces. More than once, the sexual difficulties in a marriage have been seen to be the results of relational problems not clarified. Perhaps the two cannot even tell each other how they really feel and what they need. And this, basically, is often the result of not formulating things to oneself. A certain lucidity and the courage to be oneself seem the cornerstone of any relationship that will last, but these are not easily come by at twenty, or even at thirty, forty, or fifty. Scott Peck speaks of a woman who came to him for analysis but always combed her hair afterward because she did not want her husband to know she had been on the couch. This author comments that the analysis will be successful when she no longer minds her husband knowing—in other words, when she can be herself with him.[2] This story is significant for many human situations.

If human life is about individuation, why all this fuss about relating, about building community? Jung will be cited on this issue in a later chapter, but for now it is important to note that true relating is possible only out of one's real being. The less I am an individual, the less I can open myself in truth in any relationship, and the less real the relationship will be. And conversely, the less I relate to others from the truth of whom I am, the less I will grow to be myself deeply. Guggenbühl spoke of marriage as a means toward individuation, as a call that not everyone shares. One could conclude that a marriage, to be strong, requires that people be themselves, know themselves to some degree, be willing to share what they know, and be able to open themselves to the reality of the other and of their common life, however much testing and trial such an experience may involve. And what holds of marriage holds, in differing degrees, of other forms of relationship or community. A community or family in which people cannot—or do not—share who they are and receive others as they are may well be called a "bed and breakfast" situation—it is hardly a community. And this whole question returns to that of priorities.

Is relationship truly a priority? This question applies very differently to a married couple, their children, and another type of community like, for example, a religious community. In a marriage one presumes that the relationship is indeed important and where its cultivation is not a priority some serious questioning needs to be done. Nor is caring for the house, garden, children, or finances a replacement, common as that impression may be. "I am working for you," is not the same as, "I am with you"—in any relationship at all.

For children, life in a family may seem mainly a preparation for growing up and moving out on their own. But if the love in their relationships has been insufficient in their home—love given as well as received—their later relationships will suffer. Children may not feel they must "cultivate relationships" with their parents and siblings, but if they are indifferent to these it bodes ill for the future—perhaps largely because it suggests self-centeredness, which is far from a root of individuation.

In religious communities—and in other adult communities—the primary purpose may not be to relate to each other but to live together a common purpose or ethos. Antoine de Saint-Exupéry is supposed to have said that love is not looking at one another but looking together in the same direction. Nonetheless, it is necessary to be clear about what that "together" means. Why should each person not seek that aim alone—as was done in the early days of religious life, in the deserts? What is the purpose of being together? If it is mutual enlightenment and strengthening, it is important to know whether these occur, and, if not, why not? (Often, I suspect, it is because of the risk referred to in chapter 7. But if one is not willing to run this risk, why live in community?)

Some will admit to being in community for purposes of security and ease: the group cares for finances, cooking, and cleaning, and one can even have companionship without a real effort to relate. (And more than one married woman has remained in a marriage for just such security.) But if this is the case, is there not value in calling things by their names? In a barracks there is no pretense at building community, though friendships may become very real. The needs of life are supplied so that the inhabitants may be free for outer activities. It is important to know whether one wants to live in a family, a community, or a barracks, and what the differences are.

What is a community, as opposed to a barracks? Part 3 will investigate some other authors' views on this point, but for now a few more things about priorities need to be said.

It is my belief that neither a marriage nor a community can survive if all the priorities are external. If the purpose of one's life is to make money—or to do good, or to be successful, or even to change the world—then one needs to know that any marriage, relationship, or community will only be of importance insofar as it is a shoulder-to-shoulder working to that end. And when the other ceases to be helpful, doubtless one simply goes on alone. The other is relatively incidental. (Or does one try to "do good" to the other? I still remember the rage of one marvelous old nun when another apologized for "giving her bad example." "Don't try to give example to me," she fumed!)

What differentiates marriage, relationship, community from organizations like the above is the conviction (far more often implicit than explicit) that the other with whom I live has within him or her something of the divine (as in the story that concluded chapter 7), though many spouses would not use such language. If I also have something of the divine—or, since one does not "have" the divine, if something of the divine dwells in me—then the place where we live together is holy ground. This brings a call to reverence this place—not the physical location but the "place" that is this community—as a place of revelation. In the other I find something of God and I learn something more than I know; I am stretched (perhaps painfully) beyond where I would have gone. I meet my shadow; I meet contradiction and the defeat of my individualism and selfishness. And perhaps, if it all bears fruit, I meet love. In the ancient Egyptian deserts, people went out to seek God in solitude. They were not seeking relationship or community. Even they soon discovered their need for the wisdom of an other who had already walked this way, and they learned that solitude requires an apprenticeship. In this apprenticeship they learned to obey and revere that other in a way unheard of in most circles today. Even not seeking relationship or community they learned the pitfalls of walking alone, the need to value the wisdom and gifts of another, and the "unselving" that results from such openness. The thought bears reflection. We make our journeys toward individuation, God, or whatever goal we seek with others to a greater or lesser degree. It would be important to understand what this phenomenon really means in terms of reverence toward who that other is as well as who I am.

In other words, even if people embarking on marriage do not speak of meeting the divine in the other, that is what occurs. Falling in love involves projecting onto the other some of the numinous in oneself,[3] which one must learn later to recognize as one's own if there is ever to be recognition of the other as who he or she really is. But that real being is no less numinous than mine. When Christian tradition speaks of marriage as symbolizing the union of Christ and the church (or Christ and the individual psyche), it draws on an insight of the Hebrew tradition, as seen in the Song of Songs. (This insight is shared by other traditions as well, of which more in the story closing this chapter.) Theresa of Avila once remarked that if one could really see another "soul," one would kneel in adoration thinking it to be God.[4] Perhaps marriage and community are about coming closer to this awareness.

It is important for me to say that I do not exaggerate the benefits of community. I have quoted St. Basil's saying, "If you are a hermit, whose feet will you wash?" The implication is that community is better than solitude. Much of Western monasticism, however, sees the hermit's as the highest life—as Hinduism sees the sannyasi's life as often following the householder's—and psychologically, Jung's stress on individuation might seem to go the same way. Perhaps one of the best comments I know is Bonhoeffer's quotation that only one who loves community is safe living alone, and only one who loves solitude is safe living in community.[5] This would seem to me to be because community is an excellent area for the purification of selfishness, and if one lives alone out of selfishness, it is to be wondered what the effects on eventual individuation could possibly be. So calling this chapter "Priorities" is not meant to place community as a priority in itself. But it is meant to say that *if* one chooses to live in a marriage or in a community, it is important to be willing to pay the price of the reverence and "unselving" that result when the choice is really lived.

The story with which I wish to end this chapter is about the divine nature and symbolic meaning of marriage and of any true relationship. These are beautifully rendered in Rabindranath Tagore's play, *The King of the Dark Chamber,*[6] which should really be seen or read in the original rather than read in a summary which sacrifices much of the symbolism and beauty. In this play, a princess marries an exalted king whose one requirement, in exchange for all he gives his bride, is that she not ask to see his face but rather meet him always in a dark chamber. His people, also, never see him, though the country prospers. Obviously, each one's image of the king and questions about him are born of personal inner issues—we would say "projection." For a long time the princess, now queen, complies with the king's demand, but finally, disconcerted by the questions of others (including some plotters) who ask whether it is ugliness or some other reason that makes the king require such a thing, she asks to see him. He warns her, but she insists; so he promises to walk out among the people on the following festival day.

Looking from her balcony, the naive young queen sees a beautiful young man set up by the plotters to impersonate the king, and she believes it is her husband. Disillusioned to learn just how bad her error is, and after a fire in the palace from which she tries to flee to this scarecrow king for help, she feels deep shame. In the crisis she does see the true king, but finds him too dark and terrible to bear. She loves the bright beauty of the imposter and flees home to her father's house. The plotters against the king, royal themselves, take her father prisoner and require, in order to free him, that she choose one of them to marry. She is convinced the king will send her rescue and call her back. The rescue comes, but the king does not call her back. Only when she is ready humbly to return, uncalled for and acknowledging her error, walking the dusty road to seek him in a new knowledge of herself, life, and him, does the king receive her with love and forgiveness. Now, that she can bear who he is and who she is as well, they can go together out into the light.

This brief sketch is a real injustice to Tagore's story. It conveys, however, some of what the author is trying to say. The other—like the Other—is always seen in a dark chamber, and often we cannot bear his—or our—reality unveiled. We prefer what is visible and attractive and, seeking this, find ourselves in the worst kind of danger. Rescue does not spare us the need of a humble mendicant contact with our own poverty and need for forgiveness. With a spouse, a friend, a brother or sister, we meet the king in the dark chamber. Not in illusion but in poverty and humility we come to know ourselves and him. Community, friendship, and marriage have many "secondary gains." But if ultimately one does not come to this meeting wanting and giving something more than these, the deepest meaning of the whole situation has not yet begun to be found.

· 12 ·

FIVE *S*'s:
SOLITUDE, SEXUALITY, SPACE,
SHARING, STABILITY

No, this chapter title is not a gimmick. Increasingly I believe that the interplay of the above five elements can make or break a community, marriage, or family. As a starting point for this reflection, I would like to take a comment made by a woman recognized in her circle as something of a wisdom figure. She is a wife, mother and grandmother, with extensive experience in the varied communities her very rich life has touched. When I told her I was writing about community, she remarked that community was a subject of crucial importance today. Asked why, she added, "Community is a problem for everyone today. We think community is being together and so we try to do that, instead of understanding that community requires relatedness. We flee from this latter and its demands by putting up our plexiglass walls, and then we wonder why we are lonely."

This remark struck me deeply. One senses in it so much of the groping and loneliness on which person after person—in therapy or not—will comment. For many, the risk of breaking down the wall seems to many just too much to bear.

Sharing

In his book on the religious life, Robert McAllister, M.D., remarks, "Community entails not only a sharing of goods or labor

120

or goals, but also a sharing of oneself, emotionally, intimately."[1] However, as he points out, communities that begin thus may change in their orientation. Some religious orders began with such sharing but soon lost it. Marriages that begin with the love of two people can turn into situations where the parents are concerned with making money—or with spiritual or ethical goals and projects—and the children, as well as the unconscious parents, are left emotionally starved. In Jungian terms, Eros—which is about relatedness and not just the erotic—is left out.

"Do some communities offer more to their members than they can give?" asks McAllister. People join together out of love but establish lofty goals and do not tend this love, which then dies, he adds. But he also points out the psychological effects of the dream of the perfect family or community, which was mentioned above as the longing for the earthly paradise.

> Community claims to be the first kin of family, the promise of perpetuating the warmth of previous family ties, or the hope of discovering the affection that family never gave. Most communities, whether they are parish communities, neighborhood communities, or religious communities, cannot furnish to others what they have not found for themselves. These communities are not formed out of mutual affection and understanding, or through emotional bonding. Instead, definite decisions and practical objectives bring them together.[2]

Family-type communities, on the other hand—and these are not only families—are based on love. They continue to be such only as long as mutually loving relationships exist. Otherwise they become something else.

Modern religious communities, McAllister believes, cannot be such a kind of community. They are not based on mutual love, nor should they promise their members such an experience. "To suggest to members of religious communities that bonds of emotional love and mutual affection make up an integral part of community relationships creates confusion and disappointment. To offer aspirants such promises represents either deceit or poor judgment."[3]

McAllister comments on the "sharing groups" involved in some formation processes:

> The directors express the expectation either openly or implicitly that those in formation should perceive this group as a kind of

family unit, a loving group of friends whom one can trust and with whom one can engage in limitless self-disclosure. It would be nice if it were so. A person does not come to trust others based on studying together, living together, praying together, or having a common superior or director. Those who work in marriage tribunals recognize that couples may live together for years and never establish a relationship of mutual trust.[4]

It takes time to build up trust, he adds—for any individual, let alone a group. Sharing one's inmost feelings when such trust is not yet present seems to him sheer indiscretion, a kind of public disrobing. Even family members need to respect one another's space, he adds. And he quotes a high school student's comments on a retreat in which people shared "private thoughts and family secrets in an atmosphere of lighted candles and hand-holding closeness." The student compared this experience to a one-night stand.

McAllister speaks of the illusion found in some religious communities which think that a small group choosing each other can find such intimacy. He traces the evolution of such groups—at least possible evolution—partly in terms of jealous refusal to allow outside relationships to members in order to safeguard the group's intimacy. To him, ability to be open to others is a test of healthy relating.

His suggestion is that religious communities stop claiming to produce anything like family affection or intimacy and base their unity on spiritual motivation that brings them together. As for families, when relating ceases to be based on love and is more a question of duty and responsibility, he suggests honesty here as well—less in terms of being brutal about what is than in terms of not pretending to or speaking of a love that is not. The issue is one of realism.

The whole question, for him, touches that of celibacy. Married life provides emotional and physical intimacy, he says, while celibate life does not. Choosing such a life should be done lucidly and without illusion.

Does his opinion conflict with the one quoted in opening the present chapter? Does it conflict with Guggenbühl's remarks on the importance of being able to share even "kinky" sexual tendencies and fantasies with one's partner, lest one try to force oneself into a mold that is no longer personal or true to who one really is?

I believe that there is a conflict between the first two views.

While I value the perspicaciousness of much in McAllister's comments, I think there is probably very considerable middle ground between the kind of sharing possible only in intimacy and very deep trust and the coolly goal-oriented attitude he seems to recommend as realistic for religious and other such community groups. His remarks about the place and importance of relationship seem to me to be the key. He is right in saying that communities cannot furnish to others what they have not found for themselves. In other words, if a community does not value *community as such*—that is, the values of this particular group's affective and human life together—and if this "valuing" is not efficacious and shown in concrete choices, then McAllister is right about the perniciousness of false promises and of pseudo-intimacies. And, as he also says, time for living together, some stability, time to build trust, and time to come to share appropriately are essential ingredients for the building of such relationships. We shall see in more than one example below that love is something that can, to some extent, be learned. Learned, not simply willed. It is a spontaneous grace, a gift, and also, yes, a matter of "chemistry." But where one listens to and receives and reverences another in the way discussed in the last chapter, love has a chance to grow. Some structures in community living can facilitate the kind of openness and sharing in which such love can grow. I am not, needless to say, referring to situations like McAllister's "one-night stands." Asking for a spiritual or emotional striptease is no solution.

On the other hand, if I can share nothing at all of what I am really feeling or wishing, then some questions need to be asked. Is the problem mine or the group's? And of what does it consist, in either case? Some clarity is probably possible—notably about the nature and the needs of such strong defenses—and while clarity may be painful, some pain leads to health. If there is no sharing and no honesty at all, surely the togetherness is more a travesty than anything else—or an honest bed-and-breakfast situation. Here McAllister's plea for honesty seems a real value. But it does seem possible to say that without frequent regular meetings where people can experience in depth what their life together means, community can hardly exist. Couples can do this (some do even nightly); communities can do it as well. To me it seems that this is what lays the bricks of a solid building.

Clearly it is important to understand the nature of the group and its closeness. A big city parish cannot possibly create the same kind of community atmosphere as a religious community, nor should it try. A community of seventy-five monks will be different from an apartment of three sisters, and its structures will differ. On the other hand, one cannot conclude that the group of three is necessarily more intimate. As McAllister says, the question is why they came together. And one touches here on an important problem. If a group comes together primarily out of emotional intimacy, surely it is almost necessarily going to find itself in conflict if its primary dedication is meant to be some religious ethos. Which will come first—the intimacy or the ethos of work, prayer, or whatever? We are back to the question of formulating clear priorities. The answer to this question of priority will be played out in concrete choices, concerning time especially. In the years after Vatican II some communities spent so many hours trying to "exchange" in depth that there was hardly time for prayer and certainly little for relaxation. Where does the primacy lie? On the other hand, a very large community together for the stated purpose of living a certain ethos can indeed come to create some very deep bonds, at least between certain members. These can amount to real, deep, and very humanly fulfilling love—even when certain kinds of intimacy are deliberately renounced. This love can imply the "intimacy" of deeply shared convictions, aims, and values—not little things in any relationship's life. Perhaps an important insight in this regard can be found in contemporary sociology's distinction between *Gesellschaft* ("society") and *Gemeinschaft* ("community")—the former having its interactions dictated by a purpose outside itself and the latter being built around what the group members share affectively, historically, and in terms of use of time.[5] If what calls itself a "community" becomes a "society," being aware of this fact is important.

Sexuality

All this brings us to another of our five *s*'s whose interrelatedness and interactions with each other seem to me most likely to lead to a certain clarity in all of this. Guggenbühl's idea of honesty in the sexual domain—symbolic of other forms of honesty as well—may be very appropriate in a marriage or a very deep friendship and totally inappropriate elsewhere. And yet some openness about this domain, which is part of everyone's life, is important. As regards religious communities, one essential point is the much-belabored distinction between the genital and the sexual. Religious men and women are, and need to be, men and women. To change the meaning of a contemporary phrase, they may opt not to be genitally active but how can they be human and not be sexually active in this sense of the term? If they seem very sexually frustrated or repressed, some serious questions need to be asked about their life-style. Were they, perhaps, mistaken in thinking themselves called to celibacy? Are they living their celibacy in the wrong way? What causes the impression of frustration, sourness, rigidity, and repression? If Jesus in the Gospel has a kind of archetypal significance for the religious (Jung would say, as a symbol of the Self), surely it is worth reflecting that He hardly comes across as inhibited, frightened, or frustrated in this domain. (How many of his professional followers would allow a prostitute the kind of physical expressions of affection—public at that—involved in the foot washing at Simon's house?) Perhaps His remark about food fits here as well, "I have food to eat of which you know not." Doubtless He also received love and intimacy—of which John's Gospel speaks—which those with Him did not know. If the religious life does not give someone the same kind of vibrant quality that results from a happy marriage, this may be a question of temperament. But it may also be a sign that something is radically wrong. Relationship—with God *and* relationship with others—needs to be sufficiently fulfilling for this to occur, and where this is not the case investigation is in order. Prayer can be difficult; community can be agony. Nevertheless, all this needs reflection.

Once, a famous Jesuit remarked that if prayer was hard for a long time, one should not just settle down and speak of desolation but rather one should ask what is wrong in one's life. Another religious remarked that being present to others in community—just simply physically present—was a sexual act and meant something to them sexually. I believe this, and when people now say scornfully that community is not just about being all together at the same time and in the same place, I believe—while agreeing—that it is important to balance this view with the one just given. A woman or man living with others—in theory—but in fact always feeling alone without wanting to be, can be as frustrated and, in a sense, sexually deprived, as a spouse in a marriage that is going badly. As has been said again and again, sexuality needs to be considered in its wide sense to be realistically dealt with for religious—but it does need to be seriously considered. The very serious question of the "chemistry" between people, a point that can be extremely important in the setting up of community, is deeply connected with the whole question of sexuality.

A related issue is that of same-sex communities. In a world that has evolved as ours has—but even more basically, simply in terms of human nature—is it healthy to live in a purely male or female society? People who do not can become hard and unnuanced, petty and subjective—to cite only four relatively stereotyped results—as much as people who do, but Guggenbühl's remarks on the importance of dealing with the contrasexual need to be remembered. If a man is to develop his feminine side and the woman her masculine—without necessarily falling into being effeminate men and masculine women—this interior work has to be done. It can, however, help one in this development to have friendships with the opposite sex, especially if one knows how to evaluate one's projections (as chapter 14 will examine). This is no less true for the married than for religious. Married women as well as single need friends of both sexes, as do men. Richardson[6] remarks that sexuality is more a matter of communication of thoughts, feelings, and inner life than of genital contact. In this sense of the term it is important to see how the two entities—community and sexuality—relate in one's life and to know that if they do not strengthen and deepen each other, something is going wrong.

Space

When all the above has been said, however, it is time to reflect on McAllister's plea for mutual respect, privacy, and space. Personally, I believe that much in the concept of shared prayer as practiced in some circles after Vatican II can be questionable along these lines—especially when imposed in community. If a person's relationship with God is an area of the deepest intimacy and privacy, how can one be expected to share this relationship in any depth in a group of others, however Christian? Or is it meant to be like the "small talk" between a husband and wife before guests? On the other hand, shared reflection on a text or topic is another question and is surely less a violation of privacy, however threatening even this can be to some if moved out of the purely speculative sphere.

The issue of space is a basic human question, important in marriage as in religious community. If a marriage, when mature, is the relationship of two adult persons moving toward individuation, it can be expected that, with time, the need for personal space, interests, projects, and concerns will grow. This needs to be an awareness from the beginning. The notion of a total symbiotic sharing of all things is a false dream that has damaged more relationships and certainly more marriages than we can know. It needs to be recognized as such.

The same issue, for religious, seems to me remarkably unnoticed—notably in canonical legislation in the West. Early years of training give a certain orientation, even a cast to the personality—as, indeed, early years of marriage also leave a mark—but in a religious order this training can carry the weight of centuries of tradition. As a person matures and individuates, however, we have seen that there is a movement out of the collective to become one's own person. An excellent recent article speaks of the rhythm of development: early discipline can be a real value, and later one grows in freedom.[7] The Benedictine Rule speaks of a possible development toward an eremitical life. As a person grows, one should expect a movement beyond early boundaries and into new domains. This cannot be legislated. Why, in the West, is this so unexpected that many such people have either to leave their community or struggle as Merton did? One should expect an adult—married, religious, or single—to need, want, and use more space in many ways. Communities and marriages that expect this and prepare for it are wise indeed. And they can hope to be enriched in proportion to this wisdom.

Solitude

Guggenbühl speaks of a possible increase, with time, in the need for solitude as well as space. This seems a very important issue. I would like to distinguish the concept of solitude from that of space, though in fact they are very close. One has space physically when one is outside, when others (people or things) do not crowd in on one, when one has time to do—or, even more, to be—as one needs to do or to be alone.

Solitude is more about the aloneness. It can be a marvellous space where one is free at length to create, to live, simply to be. But it can also be terrible. Space gives me the chance to be who I need to be, to do what I need to do, to breathe freely without having other people or things around all the time. Solitude means going into this "space" alone and staying there until it speaks to me, until its depths emerge—be they angels or hidden dragons and wild beasts—until I have gone through the growth and struggle and journey and evolution my own soul requires. Bonhoeffer remarks that we are born alone and die alone: no one can do these things for us, nor would we want this. And we are born and die in many of our deepest choices. The tragedy is that so often we do not make these choices alone. We say—and think—we did it because X encouraged it or Y wanted it or it would make Z happy. For religious people, it may seem to fit into a corporate ethos or an ideal image of what one is trying to be. But these are not the real reasons at all. The real reasons lie in our inability to face the risks and solitude required to be personal in what we choose and do—the inability to move beyond the collective, to individuate.

This inability to bear solitude is reflected in community. Chapter 4 spoke of the value for any community of even one person who has worked through to individuation. Such a person may not be comfortable to live with at all times—notably to others who do not wish to move in that same direction. Such people are notorious boat rockers: one thinks of Socrates. But on the other hand, the person who has learned in solitude—at least the inner solitude—who he or she is and what is really going on inside can also be a great help in what he or she can formulate. In "The Teresian Contemplative," Crashaw wrote, "Our darkest guesses, dim with fears, she touches, handles, sees and hears."

Aside from what a person comfortable with solitude can give to others, there is also the question of people unable to deal with solitude. Everyone has met—in communities and out—the emotionally needy who have to clutch someone, anyone, to talk to about anything. One can feel very deep pity at such a meeting but what happened in this person's development? We cannot all be physically well and strong; we cannot be so psychologically, either. But a certain growing ability to deal with the solitude that is every person's lot is important.

It is moving to see how later life moves one into solitude. When married people lose a partner of fifty years' standing, or apostolic religious lose a ministry they have done well for years and love, what they experience is the pain of a deep loss. Still, after this pain dies down a little, what is left is a deep solitude, an aloneness. How will they deal with this? The person who has come to understand solitude goes on through this test of the later years and turns it to value. For others it can be too much to bear—and one can always try to hide behind hours of television and chatter to avoid facing this pain. Still, life itself seems to tell us of our need to make friends with solitude. And, as early writers said of the monk's cell, if one makes friends with solitude, eventually it can become dear to us and highly valued. But the cost is high.

Stability

We return to the last of our five *s*'s—stability. In terms of what was said above about sharing, and the difficulty and risk this involves if carried on at any depth, one can certainly say that it is asking too much of human nature to expect people to work toward a level of real trust and mutual sharing and then start the same process anew the following year—and each following year. More than one religious—some quite young—has spoken of the emotional exhaustion, weariness, and finally disillusionment with community that results from this process. It also leads to a half-unconscious need for inner defenses against the continual renewal of emotional strain. Yet this is something that occurs time and again in religious communities. Even where the bulk of a small group in an active community remains the same, it is very frequent indeed that there are at least some changes. A new person or two comes in—usually people who have not lived in the house before and who have been accepted because

on relatively superficial acquaintance they seemed compatible—
and the whole process needs to be begun again, and again. At
times, the new combination is happy and all goes well. Very often,
however, even if the new "mix" is good—chemically and otherwise—the newness remains for a long time and a certain awk-
wardness with it. As one religious remarked to another who had
decided not to change communities after a difficult year, "At
least if you stay it is like an old shoe." Old shoes, in such a context,
can be a real value.

There is a connected issue to this whole problem. One of the
characteristic tasks of mid-life is learning to build a stable relationship with an imperfect other or others, learning a certain
rootedness and stability. What happens to the psychological and
emotional development of people who never have a chance to
work through this task? I do not consider this question unimportant—either for religious or for others living similar situations.

These problems have no easy solution, and they are questions
that, in our age of mobility, many people who are not religious
face. Children of military or diplomatic families have always
talked about the instability in their lives. Still, these are questions
that need addressing today especially because the mobility in our
culture may have much indeed to do with the loneliness, insecurity, and unhappiness one so frequently sees, notably in the
cities. Having people around one does not make one less alone.

Some observations from Bellah's *Habits of the Heart* on the
meaning or importance of love in our culture are very relevant
here. He remarks that, "Americans believe in love as the basis
of enduring relationships," and then traces what this means in
a few sample marriages. Speaking of one which seems to have
grown quite naturally out of a high school romance, he writes:

> . . . their relationship embodies a deep sense of their own identity,
> and thus a sense that the self has found its right place in the world.
> Love embodies one's real self. In such a spontaneous, natural re-
> lationship, the self can be both grounded and free.[8]

Other couples, he remarks, need to struggle more toward a
truly loving relationship and sometimes need to be older before
finding it. One woman remarks of a husband she met under
such circumstances, "I really was able to be myself with him."

Bellah remarks, "The natural sharing of one's real self is, then, the essence of love."

These points cast an important light on our reflection of this chapter. If one applies them to religious and other communities one could say that if love is about being able to share one's real self, then ideally one would hope that communities, in the deep sense of that word (I distinguish *community* from a group meeting to do a given work), would be places where people were able to love. The burden of this lies on both the individual and the community. If one is too sensitive, too defensive, too fearful to share, then perhaps there is still not yet sufficient ability to love or to live in community. Perhaps it is necessary to get help to come to that point. On the other hand, if the community—or what claims to be such—sets up an atmosphere in which being oneself becomes unsafe and threatening, then perhaps the community itself should not yet call itself that. Perhaps it needs to work, consciously and seriously, toward deserving that name. For groups that consider community living to be an essential part of their ethos, some serious reflection on what this would mean and require is in order.

These are generalizations. Only the individuals living in a group calling itself "community" can say whether they feel free to be themselves, and why or why not. Only that group, working together, can try to see whether a difficulty is born of an individual's problem or the group's—or both, or a situation of incompatibility. But an essential point to remember in all this is Bellah's definition. Sharing is not something one demands that others be able to do. Sharing is one's own self-gift that is love. And love is about risk.

Bellah continues with a discussion on the balance between sharing and being separate. He speaks of several cases where women lost themselves in their role as wife or mother and, in losing their "self," lost "precisely the self that was loved." This could, he reflect, lead to losing one's husband. There is a kind of false mysticism (in my language) of marriage in which one dreams of losing oneself in or for the other. So the women in his examples became aware that they needed to be themselves in order to love; that they needed their own separate existence— or space—in order to be able to share at all. To use a metaphor, space becomes like the soil from which the flower of sharing or love can grow. To be a person worth loving, one must assert one's individuality. Once again we are back to the rhythm of sharing and space.

But we need to remember, before closing this section, that stability is a real value for communities—as it is for relationships and marriages—and that it needs to be recognized as such in reflection on the subject. Where this element is missing, the building of community becomes increasingly difficult. Realism here is of the very essence, and people need to realize when the very nature of community is being sacrificed by the neglect of this factor that belongs so deeply to the psychology of relationship and community. On the other hand, a certain stability in solitude is essential, too, for individuation and hence, ultimately, for community. Fleeing from oneself into television, chatter, amusement furthers nothing we have discussed above.

All these are needed then: solitude and sexuality, space and sharing, and enough stability to build relationships in some depth.

Why has the order of treatment of the *s*'s in this chapter differed from the order in the title? The chapter has moved developmentally. Community grows through sharing which can be a form of sexual expression and which develops in a dialectic with the need for space. The needs for space and solitude can begin early, but they often increase with time, as does the valuing of stability. The young often need more experience and change.

The title, on the contrary, lists the *s*'s in a more theoretical, even ideological, order. Solitude seems to me to be a prime value for individuation, but its complement is sexuality, which involves not only sharing but the Eros that is the heart of relatedness.

The pendulum swings back to space and forward to sharing—less intense experiences, in one sense, of the same dialectic. Finally, stability is like the ground in which these experiences take place.

I believe we need to keep in mind both orders of these *s*'s—the developmental and the theoretical—if we want a fuller view of the whole. Nonetheless, all five *s*'s are needed. Without these, not only community but full human living becomes impossible. Each person must find his or her own balance of needs in these domains, as must each combination of persons that is a community. But where one of these elements is seriously lacking or insufficient it seems impossible for a healthy community to emerge.

Having looked at these central questions, let us study some scholarly opinions on the subject of community.

Part Three

Scholarly
Approaches

· 13 ·

SOME ANTHROPOLOGICAL CONSIDERATIONS

One author who has done very serious work on the concept— and experience—of community from an anthropological point of view is Victor Turner. His considerations in *The Ritual Process: Structure and Anti-Structure*[1] are especially relevant. I shall follow his thought in some detail in order to see what it teaches about the phenomenon of community.

Turner addresses the subject of community in a chapter called, "Liminality and Communitas."[2] Liminality, for Turner, is "the state and process of mid-transition in a rite of passage."[3] The word comes from the Latin *limen*, "threshold," and Turner remarks that all rites of passage or transition contain three phases: separation, margin (or *limen*), and aggregation.[4] That is to say that the person undergoing a rite of passage is separated from his or her earlier place or state in the cultural whole; goes through a period of belonging neither to the old nor to the new; and finally is reincorporated into a new state in his or her social world. During the period of liminality "an intense comradeship and egalitarianism" appear among the neophytes sharing the experience. "What is interesting about liminal phenomena . . . is the blend they offer of lowliness and sacredness, of homogeneity and comradeship."[5]

It is as though there are here two major "models" for human interrelatedness, juxtaposing and alternating. The first is of society as a structured, differentiated, and often hierarchical system of

137

politico-legal-economic positions with many types of evaluation, separating men in terms of "more" or "less." The second, which emerges recognizably in the liminal period, is of society as an unstructured or rudimentarily structured and relatively undifferentiated *comitatus*, community, or even communion of equal individuals who submit together to the general authority of the ritual elders.[6]

Turner uses the term *communitas* to designate a kind of relationship essential to this experience. He remarks that the distinction between structure and communitas is not simply that between secular and sacred, since some offices in tribal society have many sacred attributes. "But this 'sacred' component is acquired by the incumbents of positions during the *rites de passage* through which they changed positions. "Something of the sacredness of the transient humility and modelessness goes over, and tempers the pride of the incumbent of a higher position or office."[7] What is this about? "It is . . . a matter of giving recognition to an essential and generic human bond, without which there could be *no* society."[8]

What is Turner saying? Basically, that there is something in common between human beings that is far deeper than our social structures and organization. This common experience is the basis of social structures, and yet it is an experience one can lose in the process of living the structures. Rituals, like rites of passage, can bring one back into contact with this more primary experience; hence their element of sacredness. Turner believes that each individual's life "contains alternating exposure to structure and communitas, and to states and transitions."[9] Without this, life would be sterile.

Turner follows in some detail the ritual by which a chief is invested with his authority among the Ndembu of Zambia. Preliminal and postliminal attributes are stripped away and the "initiand" lives as sexless and anonymous, in submissiveness and silence, hearing the reproaches anyone may wish to address to him without response. This lowliness must precede greatness: the stripping makes him "a *tabula rasa*, a blank slate, on which is inscribed the knowledge and wisdom of the group."[10] The process is meant to keep chiefs from abusing their new privileges. Continence, in this setting, is another aspect of poverty and "strippedness," since it annihilates temporarily all structural differentiation and its effects.

The significance of this whole process is to impress upon the initiand, as well as on the spectators, the fact that structure and the offices it provides are instrumentalities and gifts of the commonweal. They are not for the aggrandizement of the individual, a fact some supposedly more civilized cultures seem to forget. "Even when a man has become a chief, he must still be a member of the whole community of persons. . . ."[11] and must show this. Turner relates this ritual to the medieval knight's vigil, which takes place

> during the night before he receives the accolade, when he has to pledge himself to serve the weak and the distressed and to meditate on his own unworthiness. His subsequent power is thought partially to spring from this profound immersion in humility.[12]

In other words, for Turner what all this experience teaches is a double condemnation of "two kinds of separation from the generic bond of communitas": abuse of one's office and the following of one's urges at the expense of others. "A mystical character is assigned to the sentiment of humankindness" here, and "in most cultures this stage of transition is brought closely in touch with beliefs in the protective and punitive powers of divine or preterhuman beings or powers."[13] What is being said, then, is that power and authority must remain in touch with their roots in the human commonality, and that this process will help maintain both a sense of the imperatives of virtue and justice and a connection with the divine. Perhaps it is important to remember not only that one is human but also that one can be less than human. One thinks of the Christian Ash Wednesday ritual, which reminds people that they are dust, as well as of the flaming brush always carried before the papal throne with the words, *"Sic transit gloria mundi."* These are not merely pretty customs or quaint folklore. If one follows Turner's thought, they are essential reminders of our common heritage with all other human beings, our common bonds.

Turner lists the factors that distinguish the liminal situation from the structured system. In the first one finds communitas, equality, absence of status and property, sexual continence, humility, unselfishness, obedience, sacredness, sacred instruction, silence, foolishness, simplicity, and an acceptance of pain, as contrasted with their opposites in the structured system. He observes that many of these properties go with what Christians and others call religious life, and he concludes that what happened with Christianity and other religions was that what in itself is a "passage" for all became an institutionalized state. "Nowhere has this institutionalization of liminality been more clearly marked and defined than in the monastic and mendicant states in the great world religions."[14]

In other words, a human experience of something that began as a ritual expressing an essential rootedness of human life in society became, with time, established in permanent and institutional forms. The risk would, of course, be that, in this transformation, the liminal experience would lose some of its essential characteristics. One thinks of the wealthy medieval abbeys—yet even in them, some were surely living the liminality discussed above.

What happens when, in a given religious life (whether "professionally" religious or otherwise), the focus shifts from being and life to works? One can maintain the characteristics of liminality, as did Francis of Assisi or Charles de Foucauld, but for these the main accent was not really "works" or action. When it is, suddenly one must deal with societal structures. To return to Turner's list, then, what happens to absence of status, humility, obedience, accents on the sacred, silence, foolishness, and simplicity? (There are rare cases where both accents seem combined—as in the case of Mother Teresa of Calcutta—but discussing this latter example would take us too far from our present line of thought, and the test of time will be important here.) The question is a very serious one as it implies that there may need to be a choice between the "liminal" and the structured for action—not on the level of the institutionalization of the orders just discussed but on the still deeper level of life choices. Being liminal does not help a person function in society, nor is that its meaning. Perhaps a liminal period might be of value, but in many contemporary religious communities and lay spiritualities even this seems to be questioned. Turner's reflections might be a help toward clarifying the choices to be made.

All this also touches deeply the notion of community. Is community a place where these "liminal" values—those which all human beings hold in common on their deepest level—are lived? Or is it a place among others out of which one operates in a structured society? These are very serious questions and choices. If one decides that the community is, indeed, to be liminal and counter-cultural in its values, can this be compatible with using it for a springboard to ordinary professional activity?

As one example of this state of liminality institutionalized, Turner quotes Benedict's *Rule for Monasteries*, with its emphasis on community (which, in some translations, is even considered to be the vow of *conversio morum*), self-discipline, prayer, work, family spirit lived under the absolute control of an abbot, poverty, abstention from marriage, austerity, silence, and the rest. He notes the resemblance of some of these accents with those found in the installation rites, circumcision rites, and other "passages" among the tribes he has studied. Above all, in both cases, there is a cutting across the lines of all societal distinctions. No one is preferred above another for social reasons. Turner notes Goffman's remark in *Asylums* that these are the characteristics of those living in "total institutions," which then paradoxically produce a liminal kind of life-style.

Mysteriously, Turner points out, these liminal roles are experienced by society as dangerous, though they are also permitted what is not allowed to others. From his position outside the common social order, the court jester may say to the king what no one else may.

> Members of despised or outlawed ethnic and cultural groups play major roles in myths and popular tales as representatives or expressions of universal-human values. Famous among these are the good Samaritan, the Jewish fiddler Rothschild in Chekhov's tale "Rothschild's Fiddle" . . . and Dostoevsky's Sonia, the prostitute who redeems the would-be Nietzchean "superman" Raskolnikov, in *Crime and Punishment*.[15]

Such persons, he remarks, represent Henri Bergson's "open" (as against "closed") morality. The marginal, the liminal, then, can come to symbolize "what David Hume has called 'the sentiment for humanity,' which in its turn relates to the model we have termed 'communitas.' "[16] One finds, in this context, the prophetic role of communitas—an uncomfortable position at best, and meant to be such.

> Communitas, or the "open society," differs in this from structure, or the "closed society," in that it is potentially or ideally extensible to the limits of humanity.[17]

But, of course, movements that begin thus become institutionalized with time. It is interesting that in some of the tribes he studies Turner finds that

> The patrilineal tie is associated with property, office, political allegiance, exclusiveness, and, it may be added, particularistic and segmentary interests. It is the "structural" link par excellence. The uterine tie is associated with spiritual characteristics, mutual interests and concerns, and collaterality. It is counterpoised to exclusiveness, which presumably means that it makes for inclusiveness and does not serve material interests. In brief, matrilaterality represents, in the dimension of kinship, the notion of communitas.[18]

Where social structure is based on the masculine, he adds, it is the feminine that symbolizes links with the wider community of the human. In some tribes there is a priesthood associated with this female line—a priestly function mystically related with the whole earth and furthering peace as against feud. In another example, a matrilineal tribe views the male-to-male line as more connected with the gods. "Once more we meet with the structurally inferior as the morally and ritually superior, and secular weakness as sacred power."[19]

In summarizing the first chapter on communitas, Turner remarks, "For me, communitas emerges where social structure is not."[20] He quotes Martin Buber:

> Community is the being no longer side by side (and, one might add, above and below) but *with* one another of a multitude of persons. And this multitude, though it moves towards one goal, yet experiences everywhere a turning to, a dynamic facing of, the others, a flowing from *I* to *Thou*. Community is where community happens.[21]

This passage contains two very important concepts: that of the flowing from I to Thou and that of the statement that community is where it happens. (We shall return to these below.) The concept of community is hard to pin down, remarks Turner, because it has existential value, while that of structure has cognitive value. Yet structure could not exist without this "emptiness at the center"—and, one might add, vice versa.

Community breaks in through the interstices of structure

> in liminality; at the edges of structure, in marginality; and from beneath structure, in inferiority. It is almost everywhere held to be sacred or "holy," possibly because it transgresses or dissolves the norms that govern structured or institutionalized relationships and is accompanied by experiences of unprecedented potency.[22]

Instinctual forces are involved, he adds, but so are rationality, volition, and memory. "The notion that there is a generic bond between men, and its related sentiment of 'humankindness,' are not epiphenomena of some kind of herd instinct but are products of 'men in their wholeness wholly attending.' "[23]

Those living in community seem to require, sooner or later, an absolute authority. . . . Communitas cannot stand alone if the material and organizational needs of human beings are to be adequately met. Maximization of communitas provokes maximization of structure, which in its turn produces revolutionary strivings for renewed communitas.[24] The dialectic of structure and communitas is essential, however.

Turner now moves to two examples of this process. For working purposes he now defines communitas as "a relationship between concrete, historical, idiosyncratic individuals . . . [who] confront one another rather in the manner of Martin Buber's 'I and Thou.' "[25] He distinguishes between (1) existential or spontaneous communitas—a "happening"; (2) normative communitas, where existential communitas is organized into a perduring social system; and (3) ideological communitas—a utopian model of society based on existential communitas. (I have shortened Turner's definitions.) The last is trying to describe the first. Normative communitas is found, for example, in tribal initiation rites. Ritual may require such norms. But Turner will speak now of religious movements, and he notes the importance of absence of property in the maintaining of equality here. He also cites Buber's conviction that only one capable of saying "Thou" can truly say "We." "It is enough to prevent the *We* arising, or being preserved, if a single man is accepted, who is greedy of power and uses others as a mean to his own end, or who craves of importance and makes a show of himself."[26] Turner does not agree with what seems Buber's dream that spontaneous community can be expressed in a structural form. Some groups—hippies, or some church groups—try to "produce" the experience of communitas on a deep level and for some of these the experience is an end in itself. But, remarks Turner, it may be wiser to see this experience as a help toward the ordinary business of human living "for human beings are responsible to one another in the supplying of humble needs, such as food, drink, clothing, and the careful teaching of material and social techniques. Such responsibilities imply the careful ordering of human relationships and of man's knowledge of nature."[27] Distance, then, can be as important as intimacy. Life is a dialectic of both, and clinging to only one is not the path of wisdom. Structure without communitas is dead; communitas without structure is a magical experience, but one separate from the details of daily life.

It is important to see what happens when the experience of communitas or its ideal begins to be lived out in the world of daily reality. Turner traces this experience in the case of the early Franciscans, using as a text M. D. Lambert's book, *Franciscan Poverty*. Francis, goes the line of reflection, thought in symbols, images, and parables, and he valued dreams. Legislation, especially for large numbers, was not his forte. And he was in love with poverty, lived to the furthest extreme the brothers could manage. Material insecurity was a life choice; nakedness a central symbol. For Francis,

> religion . . . was communitas, between man and God and man and man, vertically and horizontally, so to speak, and poverty and nakedness were both expressive symbols of communitas and instruments for attaining it.[28]

As the order grew and had to be structured, much in this vision could no longer be lived. Buber dreamed of building a large community of many small communities. Such was not the legislation for religious orders in the medieval church. Still, it was ultimately the choices of the friars themselves that brought change. Rarely is everyone in a community "bitten by the original bug" quite as deeply as the group's founder. Within twenty years things had already radically changed for the Franciscans, and their founder lived apart with a small group—once again, a communitas. The order split into two branches, one more radical about poverty than the other. But even the radical branch had to develop definitions and a theology—with some of which it seems to have painted itself into a corner. It appears that communitas as such—as an experience that arises spontaneously—is necessarily transient. Structure becomes important.

In a final chapter Turner speaks of the importance of moments of "status reversal"—moments when one returns briefly to the experience of communitas. "Paradoxically, the ritual reduction of structure to communitas . . . has the effect of regenerating the principles of classification and ordering on which social structure rests."[29] The ideal would be "the notion of a perfect synthesis of communitas and hierarchical structure,"[30] as represented, for example, in the writings of Dante and Aquinas, where, "equality and hierarchy were . . . mysteriously one."[31] Many ceremonies and rituals—like our Halloween, for one, "represented a seasonal expulsion of evils, and a renewal of fertility associated with cosmic and chthonic powers."

> Somehow, as dramatists and novelists well know, a touch of sin and evil seems to be necessary tinder for the fires of communitas—although elaborate ritual mechanisms have to be provided to transmute those fires from devouring to domestic uses. There is always a *felix culpa* at the heart of any religious system that is closely bound up with human structural cycles of development.[32]

One can hardly, in this context, avoid thinking of Jung's reflection on the importance of integrating the shadow. Turner remarks that communitas cannot exercise social control but it can, "through brief revelation, 'burn out' or 'wash away'—whatever metaphor of purification is used—the accumulated sins and sunderings of structure."[33] He concludes with a thought-provoking separation of religions into two basic kinds: those that emphasize "humility, patience, and the unimportance of distinctions of status, property, age, sex, and other natural and cultural differentiae. Furthermore, they stress mystical union, numinosity, and undifferentiated communitas." Others, on the contrary, emphasize "functional differentiation in the religious sphere."[34] The liminality of the structurally superior, he remarks, is weakness; that of the structurally weak is strength. There are rituals of humility born of religions seeking these values, and rituals of hierarchy, born often among the structurally inferior— based, also, more on force than consensus. Both these rituals, he remarks, reinforce structure, but they balance its effects. People seek in ritual liminality that of which they are starved in daily life—be it humility or power. This suggests the importance of the ritual element in our lives.

What do these anthropological observations say about the subject of our previous chapters? Perhaps our reflection can begin with the question of religious community and then proceed to marriage, family, and other groups.

In the case of religious community, one obvious conclusion connects with some of McAllister's ideas, as discussed in chapter 12. To imagine that the almost mystical experience of communitas described in what Turner calls liminal situations can continue through the years and in necessarily structured settings is to open oneself to disillusionment. The question is, however, rather more complex than that. Did the groups around Francis remain communitas? How, and at what price? I would suspect that the groups around Francis did, indeed, remain communitas until the end of his life, because they were small natural groups— natural in the sense of being composed of people in love with the charism he represented, and, doubtless, attracted to him as a person as well. One imagines the group continuing after his death, but with a sense of surrounding an aching void.

What this would mean is that communitas is not entirely about "chumminess" and compatibility, though a certain deep-level compatibility is, indeed, important. Communitas is something more. A group of friends living together may experience communitas—as, also, may a group of people who have long worked together in an office or other setting. But the communitas itself is something that happens spontaneously—and can be lost.

The liminal element of which Turner speaks, however, adds another dimension that one could perhaps call sacred. Society is structured; it fulfills certain aims. But when one moves outside these structures into the other world of ritual, poverty, or symbolism and imagery, one moves into another dimension. This is the world of communitas.

Can one live in this way? Francis probably did. Benedict was already structuring the monastic life in his Rule, though he stressed the liminal values of poverty, humility, love, and the rest. This life was very much structured around ritual, so that one has, here, both ends of the equation. One imagines that there was less communitas at Monte Cassino in daily experience than there was around Francis, but one also thinks of certain moments of ritual or "charismatic" intensity when the experience of communitas must have been equally intense. Benedict's communitas was based far less on compatibility than on shared liminal experience. Therefore it seems more transient. But, over the years, it doubtless built a deep and enduring communitas on a more profound level. One thinks, in this connection, of a marriage that has continued for many years—through vicissitudes and pain and doubts and times of celebration and joy. This, too, builds in the end when both members truly participate in terms of who they are.

Communitas, then, cannot be commanded. There is even a sense in which it cannot be "built." Are "community-building" weekends, marriage encounters, and all such experiences, then, illusory? Participants know they are not. They *are* liminal experiences in which one withdraws from the pace and structures of ordinary life and its status symbols to be simply equal and to share as persons. Such an experience in itself is communitas. It can then affect the more structured daily routine that follows. Still, there is a gratuitous element in the whole experience. Communitas is gift.

Can one structure community—or a marriage? Or is reflection on mutual interests, common background, and compatibility unimportant? The question answers itself. The essential is, however, to know that when this structuring, this work of reason and common sense, is done, communitas still cannot be commanded. Two people can seem, on paper, an ideal couple. But they can meet, and something simply does not click (or even clicks negatively). The question of chemistry can never be neglected. The same is true of other communities, religious or otherwise. But then, if one has done the human part of one's homework and seen that these people should normally be compatible and that, when they meet, they experience themselves as such, this is still only half the battle. For if they do not share the spiritual kind of experience Turner discusses—be it sporadically or on a much more frequent level—any deeper form of communitas may well be slow to happen. Bellah's remarks on sharing as an expression of love should be remembered here. But even sharing is not the same as some of the ritual experience of which Turner speaks—the entering into poverty, nakedness, humility, and all the attendant elements. This "mystical" dimension is something missing in many lives— and in many communities, even religious—in our culture, and for want of it, communitas may truly die. One Roman Catholic community of my acquaintance found itself asked, surprisedly, by a non-Catholic therapist: "Don't you ever share about the things you believe in?" In this particular case, the answer at time of asking was no. The therapist's surprise was very natural, for one can return to the early question of this book: Why do members of religious communities today live together? (And the question is appropriate for marriages and families, too.) Is it only for a roof over one's head and cooked meals? Is it because one wants a base for outside work? Is it because of a shared faith and conviction lived out together—and, in this case, how are they lived together? How is all this concretely spelled out? What does a real interest in living community mean? As McAllister remarked, sharing only the same interest in work or an exterior aim can mean the house is affectively empty. Religious communities may not be together for purposes of intimacy, but if their only common interests are outside, there can hardly be communitas. And this holds also for a family.

The whole issue touches the question of the socioreligious significance of community. Is religious (or marital) community meant to be the kind of respite from and energization of the structured world of which Turner speaks? If so, it is important to see that the salt not lose its savor. And this would doubtless occur if all the values of the people involved are in this structured world and cease to be liminal. There is also a still deeper significance to communitas in Turner's terms. If communitas is about the awareness of what all people have in common—with each other and in their relationships to the earth, to nature, and to

God, long before one gets into societal issues and structures—then it is an important element to keep present in our worlds and lives. Communities living this would indeed need to remain in touch with their inner equality, need to live lives of simplicity and awareness of nature, the cosmic world, and God. This could be quite a challenge, but it is one that certain committed families are ready to face. Communities might wish to see to what extent they desire such commitment.

In order to sharpen awareness of what some of this could mean for the subject at hand, a few basic questions can be formulated.

(1) Is community—notably religious community—meant to be a liminal experience, at least in some ways? Are poverty, simplicity, equality, and other counter-cultural values important here? Is community meant, thus, to be a living of the universal human brother- or sisterhood that preceded and is the "ground" of structured society? If so, what follows from this fact? Or is community, on the contrary, simply part of today's society structures? Clarity on this issue is important for each community.

(2) The same question can be asked in another, perhaps deeper, form. If a community is meant to have something of this liminal nature, where is the element of the sacred, the symbolic, in its life? And aside from this kind of contact with the sacred, are there moments in this community's life where each person also listens, in reverence and silence, to all that others may want to say—either about themselves or even including reproaches to themselves? The older orders structured such experiences and have now revised these structures. But now—in a community or even a family—there needs to be such moments of humility, listening, simplicity, and mutual honesty. Where there are, surprising growth can result. And issues around the misuse of power can be clarified as well.

(3) Turner refers to the great monastic and mendicant orders as an "institutionalization of liminality." Where do modern religious communities see their life in this light?

(4) If one moves on to the social significance of community, to what extent—notably for religious communities—does their prophetic meaning for the world around them depend on their choice to be liminal and live the corresponding values? If some make different choices, of what do they, then, wish to speak? Marriages can certainly speak to the world of other values than

the liminal, though some families live liminal values very deliberately. Are some religious communities today deliberately "nonliminal"?

(5) If community is about "a flowing from I to Thou," is this quality of life and relationship a factor furthered by the way they live? One hopes it is in marriages and families. Is it in communities? Where this is not the case, what went wrong, or where are these dimensions supplied?

(6) Finally, how do communities, marriages, and families formally or informally structure the interplay between the liminal and the "ordinary," the moments of greater sacredness or depth and the "nitty-gritty" of daily life? Turner has pointed out the importance of this dialectic. The first without the second is unreal; the second without the first lacks soul.

All this is important because Turner speaks—without using this word—of the *prophetic* role of liminal persons. The one living outside the structures of society, free from its imagined needs for wealth, power, and prestige, by that very fact becomes a kind of ombudsman, a gadfly like Socrates, a prophet. This is not a comfortable position. In this sense, liminal communities are not comfortable either. If one is very comfortable, reflection may be needed.

A final word on Buber's understanding of community and its requirements. If only one who can say "Thou" can say "We"— and if these qualities are seen only a person free from the need to dominate, control, manipulate, and have much attention— perhaps religious communities as well as marriage and family counselors need to take a serious look at the degree of psychological and human maturity and health of people seeking such commitment. None of us is in perfect health and perfect freedom from such tendencies—far from it. But is there at least the willingness to work with these shadows and admit them? Often the fragility is too great, and then appropriate decisions need to be made. Not everyone needs to live every aspect of life. But sometimes the most fragile can be the most loving. Sometimes, also, those who seem incapable of love or redemption present us with the greatest surprises. In Christian terms, only God can judge. But humans need to be lucid about what they undertake in committing themselves to another (or to an Other). Buber provides good material for reflection. For surely, if there is one important thing to learn in life, it is the ability to say "Thou."

· 14 ·

INSIGHTS FROM C. G. JUNG

If the reader will bear with the effort of following a difficult line of reflection to its end, I believe that some important insights on the meaning of community will emerge. In a study called "The Psychology of the Transference—Interpreted in Conjunction with a Set of Alchemical Pictures,"[1] C. G. Jung reflects on a set of medieval pictures and their text. The original text concerned the subject of the mystic marriage as seen in an alchemical context, and this may be an important place to say that Jung's interest in alchemy centers around the fact that this forerunner of our modern science was far more than simply an attempt to make gold. It also presented a paradigm for the process of transformation, a process Jung sees as applying first of all to the human psyche. To him, some of the alchemists projected onto matter processes that, in fact, were psychological in their deepest sense. Much that the alchemists wrote, however, did show awareness of this spiritual/psychological dimension, some of it taken to very great depth. If we follow Jung's thought, this point will emerge.

The work Jung studies in "The Psychology of the Transference" is a set of ten pictures illustrating the "Rosarium Philosophorum."[2] The pictures represent a series of stages in the mystical marriage, from the first greeting to the union itself, through death, the "return of the soul," and the new birth. We will not stop here to explain the meaning of these expressions for the alchemists or for Jung, for the chapter of most importance for our present purposes is the second, which is called "King and

Queen." In the picture here commented upon the king and queen are standing with their left hands joined and their right hands each holding a branch. These crossed branches are, in their turn, crossed from above by a branch held by the Holy Spirit in the form of a dove. Jung remarks on the suggestion of incest in the union of left hands and will elaborate on this concept throughout the chapter.

The text accompanying the picture says that all error in the alchemical art arises when the worker does not begin with the proper substance—that is, nature. For Jung, this emphasis on nature is what got the alchemists in trouble with the church, (and later led to the development of natural science), and yet it is also always balanced (or contrasted) in the texts with the statement that the whole "work" is a gift of the Holy Spirit. The natural is contrasted with the artificial, and it may not be amiss in this context to point out the parallel between Jung's psychology and alchemy. Not the artificial and forced but rather the real human person is the basis of the psychological "work" each person must do. And yet, the results are always gift, grace. The human psyche does not and cannot do them alone.

Jung remarks that the desired union, or *coniunctio*, was seen as both perfectly natural and, on principle, incestuous. What does this mean?

The end of the "work" for the alchemists, was the emergence of the *Anthropos*, the "primordial Man," who is "man's totality, which is beyond the division of the sexes and can only be reached when male and female come together in one."[3] It will be remembered from the second chapter that Jungian thought speaks of the importance, in each person's development, of movement toward a more androgynous state. Here, "the revelation of the Anthropos . . . signifies much the same thing as the vision of Christ for the believing Christian."[4] As was said, the "work" is about transformation. However, as Jung points out, the texts suggest that this occurs "not *ex opere divino*" but "*ex opere naturae*," and the alchemists risked the charge of heresy on these grounds. He continues with some crucial comments on the meaning of the picture:

As regards the psychology of this picture, we must stress above all else that it depicts a human encounter where love plays the decisive part. . . . The crucial contact of left hands points to something "sinister," illegitimate, morganatic, emotional and instinctive, i.e., the fatal touch of incest and its "perverse" fascination. At the same time the intervention of the Holy Ghost reveals the hidden meaning of the incest . . . as a repulsive symbol for the *unio mystica*. Although the union of close blood-relatives is everywhere taboo, it is yet the prerogative of kings (witness the incestuous marriages of the Pharaohs, etc.). Incest symbolizes union with one's own being, it means individuation or becoming a self, and, because this is so vitally important, it exerts an unholy fascination—not, perhaps, as a crude reality, but certainly as a psychic process controlled by the unconscious, a fact well known to anybody who is familiar with psychopathology. It is for this reason, and not because of occasional cases of human incest, that the first gods were believed to propagate their kind incestuously.[5]

The incestuous union, then, is a symbol for the process of individuation and, as such, exercises a certain fascination over people's minds. What is fascinating here is what the symbol really signifies: the union with one's own deeper being from which most of us experience ourselves as separated. It is important to remember in this context that such a proposition, in the Jungian mental framework, is not as solipsistic as it sounds. What one finds in the depths of the psyche is not only oneself but the whole of the collective unconscious and, ultimately, the Archetype of the Self.

Since Jung is writing about the psychology of the transference,[6] he now traces the development of this process. The analytic process begins with a "conventional meeting" followed by a time of "familiarization." Here, the analysand projects onto the analyst fantasies originally vested in parents, brothers, sisters, or other family members. This, according to Jung, draws the doctor into the family circle and "provides a workable *prima materia*."[7] Working with the transference "gives the patient a priceless opportunity to withdraw his projections, to make good his losses, and to integrate his personality."[8] Jung hastens to add that the transference phenomenon occurs elsewhere than in the consulting room.

This last observation needs some further reflection. When, in daily living situations—work, friendship, community, family life—one acts in a transferential way, other people than analysts take on features that are not their own, or very slightly their own. Authority figures—or quite simply people with leadership—become parents, those big people who had unlimited powers when we were small, helpless, weak, and at their mercy.[9] People we live with become the bullying older brother, the whining little sister, or the younger siblings we had to take care of at the expense of being cared for ourselves. A wife becomes one's mother—nurturing or devouring, as the case may be. And so it goes.

It goes without saying that when we are conscious enough to be aware of such transferences and to work with them, the positive effects Jung mentioned can result. The woman who has not worked through her relationship with her father but projected it onto her husband can work through it now. The authority issues unsolved at home can be worked on in community. But this is possible only where there is sufficient consciousness of the transference. Where there are vast currents of unidentified emotion—resentments, fears, tension, allergies to people—whose sources cannot in any way be named, one is simply the plaything of these forces and cannot work with them in any positive way. This can even lead to the repetition, time after time, of the same self-defeating patterns.

As the title of this book suggests, shadow material, painful as it is, can be a help toward individuation—but only if one works with it, and for this, most people need help. If one is too frightened to trust another—whether friend, director, or therapist—one will find difficulty in obtaining such help. And few people are willing at first to run the risk of identifying such projections within the community or family. Courage, and confidence in the recipient of one's self-disclosure, are needed in order to act in this way; a certain amount of real maturity on both sides is also required. But given these, much personal "work" can be done.

Jung stresses that the impulses involved usually show their dark side—their shadow—first, and that it is necessary to recognize this element in our lives, by refusing to act, as he says, like an ostrich.

It is certainly no ideal for people always to remain childish, to live in a perpetual state of delusion about themselves, foisting everything they dislike on to their neighbours and plaguing them with their prejudices and projections. How many marriages are wrecked for years, and sometimes forever, because he sees his mother in his wife and she her father in her husband and neither ever recognizes the other's reality! Life has difficulties enough without that; we might at least spare ourselves the stupidest of them. But, without a fundamental discussion of the situation, it is often simply impossible to break these infantile projections.[10]

It is especially the last sentence of this quotation that I should like to stress, for many people living in marriages, families, or communities think that this living situation will simply grow by itself in a healthy way, that sitting down together—or with someone else—to talk about issues like the above with any kind of regularity is forced, stilted, and unnecessary. I think the above quotation makes a rather good case for the unreality of this view.

Speaking of the analytical relationship, Jung writes:

During this discussion the conventional disguises are dropped and the true man comes to light. He is in very truth reborn from this psychological relationship, and his field of consciousness is rounded into a circle.[11]

The same is true where this psychological work is done seriously outside an analytical framework. True, many people are not trained to help one another work in this way, but at least where the desire is present, mutual help and more objectivity can be attained.

Jung points out that the king and queen in the picture do not represent, as one might think, the analyst and the client. Rather, a male analyst is likely to be projecting his anima onto a female client, and vice versa. Seen in terms of other relationships, one might say that it is always important to be conscious of who or what one is projecting onto the other and how one is relating to this projection.

Jung uses two fairy tales to illustrate what he is saying. In both there is a question of a double marriage that prevents an unconscious incest.

In both tales the incest is an evil fate that cannot easily be avoided. Incest, as an endogamous relationship, is an expression of the libido which serves to hold the family together. One could therefore define it as "kinship libido," a kind of instinct which, like a sheepdog, keeps the family group intact. This form of libido is the diametrical opposite of the exogamous form. The two forms together hold each other in check.[12]

This last principle is extremely important, and Jung illustrates its meaning by recourse to an anthropological example. Referring to three different anthropological studies,[13] he remarks that primitive tribes are divided into two "exogamous intermarrying classes" that are ritually separated yet connected by equally ritual interdependence. One side breeds animals for the other, and the like. Jung sees the splitting of the psyche into conscious and unconscious as the "cause of the division within the tribe and the settlement."[14] The above division is matrilineal, which means that when the matrilineal is crossed by a patrilineal line of division, the settlement or tribe is divided not into two but into four. "The practical purpose of this quartering is the separation and differentiation of marriage classes [or "kinship sections," as they are now called]."[15] Incest is avoided by taking a husband or wife only from the opposite matrilineal and patrilineal group. Jung points out that this system predated the alchemical *quaternio* that he used as the basis of his discussion. He points out the ancient and also common nature of the kind of ritual symbol involved.

> The difference between the primitive and the cultural marriage quaternio consists in the fact that the former is a sociological and the latter a mystical phenomenon. While marriage classes have all but disappeared among civilized peoples, they nevertheless re-emerge on a higher cultural level as spiritual ideas. In the interests of the welfare and development of the tribe, the exogamous social order thrust the endogamous tendency into the background so as to prevent the danger of regression to a state of having no groups at all. It insisted on the introduction of "new blood" both physically and spiritually, and it thus proved to be a powerful instrument in the development of culture.[16]

There is a great deal more behind this reflection than appears on first reading. Everyone is aware of the terror of incest in our contemporary culture, and recent disclosures of the frequency of child abuse in this regard make one realize that such terror is not without its causes. One's basic repugnance on this issue stems, however, largely—though not only—from the fact that in child abuse a small, helpless, and normally trusting as well as needy individual is exploited by another, more powerful, from whom the first has a right to protection rather than exploitation. Experiencing horror at the psychological effects of such misuse is clearly justifiable.

Our emotional reactions to the incest taboo, however, reach further than this. One meets, among many people, a terror of introspection, a fear that any such process might be "navel gazing," a wish to remain consistently in what seems to them a healthfully extraverted process which can surely allow us a bit of reflection. I still remember with pain an incident some years ago when a younger friend of mine, entrenched in a maze of personal, emotional, psychological difficulties that she was trying painfully and rather unsuccessfully to sort out, was advised by someone she trusted "just to forget herself" and do something useful for others. Needless to say, the advice did not help and the confusion deepened.

What Jung is speaking of in his anthropological reflection is the importance of the balancing of the endogamous and exogamous tendencies (or, to use terms from physics, the balance of centripetal and centrifugal forces). Where the latter predominate, the "center," be it of the family, the community, or the individual person, will be lost. Where the former predominate, the connection with outer reality is equally endangered. The two must balance. If one reflects on a given family or community, this suggests some important questions to ask. Where is the center of this group? Inside the house? Or outside? If it is outside, is it truly a family or a community? On the other hand, if the center is inside, is the group closed to the outside world and, if so, how does "new blood" enter to prevent an unhealthily incestuous situation? ("Unhealthily incestuous" as opposed to Jung's statements above.)

> The idea of the incestuous hierogamos does in fact appear in the civilized religions and blossoms forth in the supreme spirituality of Christian imagery (Christ and the Church, *sponsus* and *sponsa*, the mysticism of the Song of Songs, etc.). "Thus the incest taboo," says Layard, "leads in full circle out of the biological sphere into the spiritual."[17]

Jung speaks of the gradual advances of the exogamous order,

as four marriage classes became eight and then twelve and then still more. The endogamous tendency is therefore increasingly pushed into the background, into the unconscious. This can, he observes—nay, it will—"lead to a dissociation of personality." The unconscious element is perceived as a "stranger" to the conscious and so is projected. This is his explanation for royal incestuous marriages, as in Egypt. But the queen or the goddess can also be recognized within, introjected rather than projected, and then she becomes the *anima*, "or that longing which has always had to be sacrificed since the grey dawn of history."[18] The endogamous tendency, then,

> shows itself to be an instinctive force of a spiritual nature; and, regarded in this light, the life of the spirit on the highest level is a return to the beginnings, so that man's development becomes a recapitulation of the stages that lead ultimately to the perfection of life in the spirit.[19]

This quotation seems to me of very great importance. Most of us learned in elementary biology that, in evolution, "ontogeny recapitulates phylogeny." The development of each of us in the womb recapitulates the stages of evolutionary development of the human race. Jung is telling us the same thing in the spiritual order. Each of us, in moving toward individuation, recapitulates the psychological and spiritual development of the human race. There is a kind of making whole of humanity in the process. This is one reason why this process of individuation is, to Jung's mind, one of the most important things—if not *the* most important thing—any of us can do for humankind as a whole. It is our blindness to the spiritual, our projection, and our unconsciousness that lead to the still primitive and brutal elements in our lives and societies—and communities.

To Jung the whole thought process of alchemy was a result of this projection of spiritual processes onto matter, but it also included the growing awareness that "this matter was not just the human body (or something in it) but the human personality itself."[20] And this is why he found alchemical texts so interesting psychologically.

In our present Christian culture, Jung remarks, we project the animus and anima in the expressions of dogma. In this case, these figures are "unconscious as components of personality." But since our civilization has fallen away from Christianity, the projections have "fallen away from the divine figures and have necessarily settled in the human sphere." They can be found in totalitarian ideologies. They can "have a disturbing effect on human relationships and wreck at least a quarter of the marriages." If one wishes, however, to see the positive side of this negative movement one can notice, he says, that the intolerable sides of this situation "are forcing us to pay attention to the psyche and our abysmal unconsciousness of it." The current interest in and greater awareness of psychology, then, can be the swing of the pendulum away from our gross unconsciousness and pain.

> It is possible that the endogamous urge is not ultimately tending towards projection at all; it may be trying to unite the different components of the personality on the pattern of the cross-cousin marriage, but on a higher plane where "spiritual marriage" becomes an inner experience that is not projected. Such an experience has long been depicted in dreams as a mandala divided into four, and it seems to represent the goal of the individuation process, i.e. the self.[21]

One could hardly be more hopeful about where our civilization—and we as individuals—might be going! Jung sees the growth of nations, as of the medieval brotherhoods and guilds, as a strengthening of the endogamous tendency. Where internationalization and the weakening of religion have lessened these, the result is an "amorphous mass."

> Consequently the original exogamous order is rapidly approaching a condition of chaos painfully held in check. For this there is but one remedy: the inner consolidation of the individual, who is otherwise threatened with inevitable stultification and dissolution in the mass psyche.[22]

This process must be *conscious*, stresses Jung, or the result will not be individuation but "that incredible hard-heartedness which collective man displays towards his fellow men." His conclusion is important to the whole of this book:

> the conscious achievement of inner unity clings to human rela-

tionships as to an indispensable condition, for without the conscious acknowledgement and acceptance of our fellowship with those around us there can be no synthesis of personality. That mysterious something in which the inner union takes place is nothing personal, has nothing to do with the ego, is in fact superior to the ego because, as the self, it is the synthesis of the ego and the supra-personal consciousness.[23]

Inner unity, then, "emphatically includes our fellow man." Once again, the balance of the centrifugal and the centripetal is essential.

The reflection deepens. There is one factor in transference that remains even after the projection is severed, because what lies behind transference is kinship libido.

This has been pushed so far into the background by the unlimited expansion of the exogamous tendency that it can find an outlet, and a modest one at that, only within the immediate family circle, and sometimes not even there, because of the quite justifiable resistence to incest.[24]

Jung remarks that in our present culture where the exogamous tendency so continues to expand, "Kinship libido—which could still engender a satisfying feeling of belonging together . . .—has long been deprived of its object. . . . Everyone is now a stranger among strangers."[25] It may be this kind of awareness that led to the remarks about the importance of community which have been quoted throughout this book. It is also doubtless the reason for the outcropping of so many attempts at common living and community building on their various levels. For, as Jung points out, kinship libido is an instinct. It seeks and needs its object. "Relationship to the self is at once relationship to our fellow man, and no one can be related to the latter until he is related to himself."[26]

This is a summary of much that has already been said about community. Community, relationship, are not luxuries with which one can dispense—for example, with the excuse that one tends to introversion. A failure to relate appropriately to others damages one's relationship to oneself and one's movement toward individuation—and vice versa. But to Jung the upshot is wider than that. Working with these issues of transference, projection, and relationship may be "laying an infinitesimal grain in the scales of humanity's soul." This question, and how each of us resolves it, is of importance to all humankind.

What has this chapter taught us for our reflection on community? First of all, we have learned that for almost everyone there will be an element of transference, of projection, in most of our relationships. This can be seen negatively as making us unrealistic about the other in question but it can also be seen positively as a chance to become aware of and work with this projection. We have seen that much of such work requires help, notably in the beginning, and profits greatly by verbalization. Those of us who want to make our whole journey alone and without help risk the loss of insights a more objective other can furnish. But allowing oneself such openness with another is difficult. In a family, a community, it is also important to identify such insights—at times, in discussion with the object of the transference. The implication is that a certain amount of common reflection and sharing is important. Where one's emotional reaction to a situation seems excessive, it is almost certain that ancient memories and experiences are involved. Identifying this— and, if necessary, getting help to do so—is important not only for good relating but, more important still, to one's own process of individuation. Remaining unconsciously the plaything of the emotional currents in one's life helps neither ourselves nor others.

Once again, this process implies not only one's own psychological work but also the fundamental discernment of the situation with the relevant others. The temptation to sidestep this process needs to be recognized as such.

Jung's forecast of the results of such inner and common work needs to be remembered, however, as he sees a rebirth of the real inner self as emerging from this struggle and process. The fruit of such sharing is the birth of the "true man." We become ourselves by owning our inner worlds—not only in solitude but with others. Strength is the fruit of being willing to be weak before our companions, that is, being willing to renounce our false appearance of strength.

A second important conclusion concerns the symbolic use of the incestuous royal marriage as an image of individuation, with the parallel awareness that, as our culture is terrified of incest, so it seems to fear introspection and inner "work." The question of the importance of the center follows—and that of the location of the center of each group. As was said above, if the center is outside the community, is it truly a community? But, if the center is inside, where do new life and new blood come from? To use another image, the importance of the balance of centrifugal and centripetal forces matters deeply.

A corollary to this view is Jung's conviction that if one tendency, notably the endogamous, is pushed too far into the background, the result is a dissociation of the personality. The psychological imbalance and alienation of today's culture seem to prove his point. Are individual communities and families any healthier or any less "dissociated"?

The imagery of the incestuous royal marriage remains very important. The invitation to individuation is a call to this inner marriage that can only be reached by growing consciousness of who we are and of the world we bear within us. Our projections mirror this inner world, but it is the interior work we do—as individuals and sometimes as community—that enables us to move toward this goal, this consciousness. The "marriage" requires this process. And our relationships are part of its necessary dialectic. If we neglect this movement, which Guggenbühl calls a real drive of the psyche, Jung says we must fear this dissociation of our personality. This is not surprising. Balance comes from integrating the inner and the outer, our experience and our reality. Splitting some of this off cannot help growth.

Jung's remark about psychological development as a recapitulation of the evolutionary development of the race shows the importance not only of individuation but also of community. Where a common life is primitive, barbaric, unreflective, and full of unidentified projections and unclarified emotion, one is clearly living in a primitive stage of human development as well. Where a community lives like some of the successful ones described in these pages, its life speaks to the whole surrounding culture of human possibilities. It becomes truly a sign, even a symbol. The social importance of such signs is not to be underestimated.

Jung speaks of the positive side of our contemporary social and political situation as being a greater interest in the psyche and its development. Perhaps we can see the present crisis in marriage, family, and community life as also inviting us to greater lucidity about the psychological order. An increasing awareness of the need for help along these lines may eventually result from much of our present anguish. It is to be hoped that this positive result will follow. Jung's other hope is that such pressure and pain will lead to an increasing search for individuation. Here, too, one can join in this hope.

Finally, the fruit of our learning to relate to ourselves and to others has social importance. In a world where people experience themselves as strangers (one thinks of Camus's book with that title, and of the whole vocabulary of Existentialism), such a fruit is a great sign of hope. And Jung's elucidation about kinship libido's need for an object can help in understanding the importance of community. This latter is not "frosting on the cake" with which one can dispense if one prefers to do so. It is an essential element in human living and culture, a necessary part of development. Much can be learned by looking at community living along these lines. May the look be lucid, as clarity on this subject could be a help to the whole human race.

INTERLUDE
(PLAYING IN BETWEEN)

As a woman—or rather, as a human being in this age which is becoming newly aware of feminine values—I can surely be forgiven for adding a few words on the specifically feminine perspective on community. Our scholarly theories are important, and we need to learn from them. Listening to life and experience, rather than to the structures that can hem these in, is equally important.

After speaking at length of what she calls "power from within" as contrasted with the more masculine "power over," a writer on this subject allows herself to fantasize about what a world dictated by "power from within" might be like:

> You arrive at the corporation for your meeting. The receptionist who greets you is nursing her two-month-old baby. Its crib lies beside the typewriter. She directs you down a corridor where two seven-year-olds on skateboards careen past you. The meeting takes place in a conference room with large glass doors overlooking the playground, which is equipped with slides, swings, games. One member of the committee is appointed recorder (to take notes); another is appointed to handle any crises that might arise among the children. In general, the children play well together—the older children keep an eye on the younger and intervene in any dangerous pursuits. At the end of the meeting, you set up an appointment with the Chief Executive Officer. "Friday afternoon is my time with the kids," he says, checking his appointment book. "Why don't you meet me at the zoo—we can talk this over at the monkey cage."[1]

She comments that in such a world productivity might fall—or it might be measured in terms of different values, ones more protective of life. As we become aware of what we are doing to our world, both the material and the human parts of it, perhaps such an option might not seem bad. However, it is clear that such a scenario is not for tomorrow, if for any time. Its values might, nonetheless, give us pause.

What is said in the above quotation tells us much about community as well. Structures are needed—even in an individual life. But when do our structures (or the lack of structure, which is also a structure) oppress or starve life, the human, the feminine? When do our groups—religious or otherwise—dehumanize and defeminize? I fear the question is all too real. As the same writer points out, only the willingness to sacrifice efficiency can change this.

> In a culture in which mastery is the realm of men, the male self comes to be identified with all that represents competence, control, adventure, spirit, light, transcendence of the body's dark demands. Yet that so-called freedom is actually denial—of the body, of feeling, of vulnerability and mortality.
> Denial is reinforced because our political and economic system depends on it. The structure of work, we have seen, is based on that denial.[2]

This quotation is not given in an attempt to castigate masculinity or masculine values. Rather, it is a criticism of the exclusive concentration on these values at the price of denial. In our communities and families this denial does indeed lead to efficiency, order, and productiveness, but it can destroy humanness and feeling in the process. The same writer gives a few principles to help one stay more in touch with the basic energies of life. "The first is always to begin where you are, not where you think you should be. . . . Another principle could be phrased: start grounded; end grounded. To ground ourselves means to connect with the earth, with what *is*, to start where we are, to root ourselves."[3] Communities and groups formed around certain ideals or spiritual principles seem to find it very difficult to begin in terms of what really is, what people really feel. It all seems so different from the ideal, the aim, the "spiritual." Yet, this is once again to identify totally with the masculine. And life is born only from the combination of masculine and feminine.

In a separate chapter this author speaks of people's dreams of community:

> We are all longing to go home to some place we have never been— a place, half-remembered, and half-envisioned we can only catch glimpses of from time to time. Community. Somewhere, there are people to whom we can speak with passion without having the words catch in our throats. Somewhere a circle of hands will open to receive us, eyes will light up as we enter, voices will celebrate with us whenever we come into our own power. Community means strength that joins our strength to do the work that needs to be done. Arms to hold us when we falter. A circle of healing. A circle of friends. Someplace where we can be free.[4]

Just the other side of our eyelids, she remarks, exists an America that keeps these promises. But when we open our eyes, the reality is all too different—a reality full of shadow, hatred, and fear which we must confront and try to change. This, for her, is the purpose of community, for such a confrontation cannot be lived alone. "In community, we have power to heal each other and to help each other. . . ."[5] Her conclusion is important to the reflection in this book:

> If we see our work as re-inspiriting the world, then we must be intimately concerned with preserving and creating community. We must challenge the principle of domination by resisting the destruction of communities that remain, and by creating communities based on the principle of power-from-within, power that is inherent in every being.[6]

These reflections give some insight into the profound significance of community in today's world. Past ages, with less transportation and less mobility, had different forms of family, village, and social life. Our world today is utterly different, and community is something we need to create, lest the values it fosters become totally absent in our lives. There are myriad forms of community, but without some valid forms—and we have seen how many forms can become invalid—people starve in more serious ways than physically. The importance of solitude and of the individual and his or her path are balancing factors for this importance of community, but both are crucially needed in our world.

What does healthy community look like?

> If we think of a group or a circle as a living entity, we can imagine that, like a person, it has a Talking Self, a Younger Self, and a Deep Self. It also has a structure that is determined by the responsibilities of each person and the relationships among individuals in the group.
>
> The Deep Self of a group is the underlying spirit, the sense of connection and common purpose, the bond. That bond is created and strengthened by sharing energy—working together, sharing food, touching each other, making rituals, singing, chanting, nurturing, laughing. . . .
>
> The Talking Self of a group is the thinking self, the group's ideas, policies, philosophies, and conversations. Younger Self is the feeling self, one which is often ignored in meetings. It is also the group's sense of humor, of play. A sound group must incorporate and work with all these levels.[7]

People fear to share their feelings, she comments, notably negative ones. Sharing constructive and positive feelings is easy: people are sure to approve. But about the negative ones, one tends to feel that "Only I am awful enough to feel this way." When a group atmosphere is sufficiently accepting for such feelings to be shared, people become able to meet on the level of who they really are and what they really feel—and, as a result, relationships become possible on a level impossible where people are only presenting to each other masks of conformity and social acceptability. Why are so many of our groups and families—and religious communities as well—operating on the superficial level, where being oneself in reality is impossible? Fear is the reason, one could conclude. And perhaps this is precisely the reason—in a world where fear can lead to nuclear war—for the importance of true community, for the importance of creating such a possibility for those around us. As Bellah remarked, it is on this level—and really only there—that love can be given and found.

In lines reminiscent of Turner, this author concludes:

> Rituals are part of every culture. They are the events that bind a

culture together, that create a heart, a center, for a people. It is ritual that evokes the Deep Self of a group. In *ritual* (a patterned movement of energy to accomplish a purpose) we become familiar with power-from-within, learn to recognize its *feel*, learn how to call it up and let it go.[8]

If a community or group has no common rituals, has it a soul? Has it any richness to its life? And how much of this dimension does a community need to lead to a meaningful common life? Each group decides this alone, but in our symbolically impoverished world, the question is of serious importance.

Another writer, discussing the issue of the full development of the human person—this time not only from a feminist position but specifically in terms of the negative attitudes toward sexuality that have been so strong in Christian circles—speaks of the importance of unifying Gospel perspectives with those of a healthy psychology.

These two perspectives come together when one remembers Irenaeus's famous phrase: "The glory of God is man fully alive. . . ." A part of this glory is men and women becoming fully human, fully developed in all aspects of their being. God's glory is diminished by any narrowed vision or truncated view of what it means to be a complete embodied person.[9]

While these statements are being made here specifically in terms of sexual morality, they hold of the whole affective or "feminine" sphere discussed above. If the glory of God is the human person fully alive, God is only glorified when people are able to live their full relatedness and their full affectivity in the ways discussed above.

Some of the remarks of the previous writer are echoed in this description of the Victorian age and its industrialization:

It was a time of hard work, dedication, and sacrifice of pleasure on the part of workers and even owners. In an age wholly geared to production, the economic organization needed a public morality that would encourage people to avoid pleasure, leisure, and experimental sexuality. No such rigidity in sexual life and ideals is evident in nonindustrial or preindustrial societies. Even medieval Europe made room for play and pleasure.[10]

The alternatives to such a way of living are seen specifically in terms of sexuality and of community:

> One of the functions of a faith community is to transform consciousness by giving new meaning to human action and assigning new value to human relationships. In the arena of sexual relationships, on a personal as well as on a global scale, we hope for a new sense of partnership, one in which power is balanced equitably and love is the love possible only between equals: free, mutually consenting and initiating, open to growth and development. The "charity" that characterizes a dominant-submissive relationship is being seen for what it is: a mode protective of an outdated cultural value. The Christian virtue of sexual love, on the contrary, is recognized as *reciprocally* self-emptying and *mutually* empowering.[11]

The sexual element in all human living has already been discussed. Perhaps a good definition of *community* could be formulated along the lines of the qualities mentioned in this quotation: *reciprocal self-emptying* and *mutual empowerment*. These qualities are critically important.

> An individual cannot survive as a person if his or her experience is solely that of the repression of the emotions of the true self. Such an individual remains an uneducated child, untested, undeveloped. In effect, the *person* shrivels and dies from disuse. It is sometimes necessary to overcome fear and dread to be free to love, for Love is healing. . . .
>
> The deepest Christian insight into *human* being is that it is *ens amans* ("loving being"), that is, which is unique by virtue of its power to love. . . . Love, as the tendency of the individual spirit to go out of itself to participate in the life of the other, is the key to understanding and developing the human being, as well as to understanding the process of history. After all, the goal of history is *persons in love,* or, in other words, embodied spirits in communication with each other.[12]

These lines give a key to the whole notion of community and its importance. Some people express love primarily in marriage and the family; some others live in community—though the first group may as well—and if this experience is not an expression of love then the kind of shriveling up and emotional death described above is the result. Does one really want people to be living in a community that is *Gesellschaft* rather than *Gemeinschaft*?[13] If so, it seems to me that the above quotation gives an indication of probable results—as well as of necessary means to avoid them. It is interesting that the basic insights of Christianity and of psychology on the central position of love converge. In a culture dominated by masculine values, love is not given primacy of place, but the present awakening to the feminine could come to rectify that.

Interestingly, another woman, writing this time about celibacy rather than sexuality, speaks along much the same lines when discussing the possible meaning of celibacy in the contemporary world:

> If celibacy comes to mean not simply sexual denial but a total commitment to the creation of a genuine world community and, within that global enterprise, a commitment to becoming an ever more loving human being, it will not cease to be baffling to a world largely structured by selfishness, or offensive to the proponents of unrestrained eroticism, but it will have to be taken seriously as a significant human venture.[14]

Three feminine voices—speaking from different points of view and out of different life-styles—all center around the same basic insights. And all three show not only the significance of love in human development but its place in community and, in turn, the significance of community in our contemporary world. They also show what kind of community deserves that name and what tendencies would keep a group from being a true community and source of life for its members and for the wider human community.

As fear is the obstacle par excellence for love, so is fear the major obstacle for the kind of community described in these three writings. And perhaps the distinguishing sign of a truly life-giving community—or perhaps one should say simply any community that really is such—would be that it is a place that heals and frees from fear. And perhaps that is part of the significance of new consciousness of feminine values in our contemporary world.

CONCLUSIONS

At the end of this long journey, let us see what conclusions can be pulled together from all the threads we have left hanging.

The shadow side of community—and some of the many elements of struggle and pain which one can meet—has been looked at in many case studies and at length. The effects of anger, personal problems (notably in a powerful personality), power struggles, leadership, and other factors as they can influence community have been studied. The result, contrary to what appears at first glance, is the realization that the primary issue is less the problem with which the community struggles than the challenge it provides to each individual in the house—and then to the whole—to individuate personally and to deal with the issue in a mature way, whatever that way may be. Guggenbühl's view that only certain marriages are "individuation marriages," and that living these requires both a real call and a conviction that this particular marriage is indeed a means or a help toward individuation was pointed out. This process was seen to require great openness and sharing between the partners involved. Much later, McAllister's remark that religious communities should not claim to promise intimacy was duly noted. We concluded that, nonetheless, the process of living in community becomes meaningful where it is truly seen in terms of individuation and that—whether a marriage, a family, or another type of community is involved—this level of community requires real commitment, honest sharing, running the risk of confrontation (in Guggenbühl's sense), and the willingness to be open to others.

173

Built into these views were certain conclusions concerning the choice of community members, structures, and a certain stability. Stability in profound openness with a different group each year is an unreasonable expectation and takes a psychic toll that many people eventually cannot pay. Choice of members, in light of chapter 13 and of Buber's comments, is another issue of great importance. (Again, there is a problem when, in some religious congregations, very difficult people or people with serious problems are placed in small groups and encroach upon the privacy and space of others. Even one such person can make the life of the whole group a veritable purgatory, if not hell. To question the wisdom of such placements seems justifiable, notably in groups not trained or helped to deal with such persons.)

The mention of structures was an effort to see that the kind of common reflection and sharing required by the above processes really takes place. Deep sharing can at times be improvised over the breakfast table, but only a very fortunate group has such a mood of common understanding and leisure that it never requires more structure for sharing. My own impression is that much of the expressed fear of structure one meets is precisely a fear of in-depth sharing and confrontation (again, in Guggenbühl's sense of the word). Some reflections of R. Pannikar are of interest here.

> I think an institution should be not only an organization but an organism. . . . The organization runs when there is money; the organism runs when there is life. . . . The organism needs a soul, health . . . is more than the sum of its components and no component can be replaced by an exact duplicate, because each is unique. If at all, the organism has to regenerate itself from within when it has been wounded. An organism dies when the soul departs, when the heart ceases to beat or the brain to vibrate. . . .[1]

He continues with the remark that in many contemporary religious congregations the aim is a certain work rather than the "establishment" in which members live. One needs to ask oneself, in these terms, when a group, a family, or a community really is an organism. If it is not, is it really a "community"? And if one speaks of a group as a community, one needs to be able to have some awareness of its soul, its life, the inner springs of its common being. In this sense, is the "organism" the whole congregation, so that some groups which live together are not "organisms" or "communities" at all, for lack of a local common life and soul? This question must be faced if lucid choices are to be made.

Another issue that emerged along these lines was that of trust. There is a kind of spiritual or psychological nakedness involved in sharing deeply with another or others, and it is truly a deviation (compared above to a one-night stand) to expect this in a situation where mutual acquaintance, trust, and acceptance have not yet been built. In a marriage as in a community, these take time and sharing—and, often, fun together. If one is not willing to give time to the building up of the relationships in the house—time that is different from that spent in common planning and work and even attention to children—one can hardly expect that the quality of trust just discussed can be attained. Bellah spoke of love as sharing oneself. Perhaps one criterion of love of those with whom one lives could be this kind of willingness to share. And, realistically, this needs to be combined with awareness of places where one cannot love in this way—even in one's house— at least for the present.

Is it unrealistic to expect a religious community or a family to be a place of love in Bellah's sense? Clearly, love cannot be commanded, and one cannot try to force it in the name of some ideal (notably, the Christian ideal). On the other hand, if one wants to live in love and another (or others) feels the same way, amazing results can sometimes be forthcoming. The truth of another person can be far more lovable than one thought when dealing only with externals. This is one indication of the importance of what has sometimes been called a contemplative gaze on reality—or, in other terms, an ability to listen with the heart.

Some of the issues discussed early in this book—especially those expressed in dreams and fairy tales—have a distinctly archetypal nature. Much of what touches people deeply taps into this level. If one can deal with this level, the experience can be enriching indeed. In daily life, as well, it can be helpful to know that what seems simply a struggle for personal boundaries can be a battle for inner freedom; that what seems a disagreement with authority can be about learning to tap into personal power. Learning to make these transpositions can be important in seeing the deeper significance of what appears so petty and small.

Another lesson from some of the more successful communities

is the communal significance of all personal spiritual/psychological work. What each of us becomes is a gift—or the reverse!—to those who live with us. Doing one's own inner work is of great social importance. Mysteriously—partly because of issues around the "incestuous" royal marriage discussed in the last chapter—religious people often resist the kind of inner work in question, fearing that it is selfish, self-occupied, or too personal, or fearing what they may find within. But it is only a real person who can help others—and a real person is something one has to *become*.

Still another question is that of escape. Many people fear refusing to live with a difficult person—or in a difficult situation—because they view such a choice as an escape, a lack of generosity. Occasionally, a family can make life deeply painful for the children—and adults—by refusing to face the degree of disruption caused by one member. Assessing this realistically and taking appropriate means to help the disruptive member is often the kindest solution for the individual as well as the group, but the desire to be nice and kind (or to be thought such, for the unkindness to all others can be serious) makes many resist such actions. Here, once again, there is question of integrating the shadow.

The importance of individual choice emerges throughout the case histories studied. In the case of the happier groups and families, there has been a real choice—of life-styles and of partners. And there continues to be real choice, individual as well as common. A group simply falling together and making the best of their situation is not likely to bear the kind of fruit these more intentional and deliberate groups can bear. If one reflects on the importance of choice in the individuation process, one can see the repercussions of choice, or lack thereof, on the quality of any common living.

The difficulty of facing—let alone hearing or asking for—truth, notably as others see it, has been another theme. This subject relates to the previously discussed issue of trust. A community, like a person, has difficulty placing real issues on the table for others' perusal and also, frequently, in asking for outside help. What passes for "help"—both within and from without—can be anything but that if it is lacking in sensitivity and objectivity, but the conclusion from this awareness is that one needs to choose carefully those from whom one asks help in seeking more objectivity and truth. On the other hand one of the important—as well as threatening—aspects of close relationship is that one allows others, or an other, into one's life at that level. And asking for psychological help, on an individual or common basis, is another step in this direction. Some of the above examples have shown the importance of willingness to take this risk. In other words, fear of intimacy is hardly a good preparation for either life in community or marriage, but more people than one would think feel the need to protect themselves from the risks of intimacy.

I would like to conclude this chapter with a quotation from an author who has asked himself many of the fundamental questions discussed in this book. Sebastian Moore writes:

> Spirit, inter-life, the mysterious energy that flows between persons . . . is what opens us to God. It is at once the opening of our *desire* to God and God's *point of entry* into us; our way of opening, God's way of entering. . . .
>
> The threshold of belief is that special sense of human greatness which is had in the experience of our larger, intersubjective life. And we only really sense this larger intersubjective life when we understand the intimacy between two persons as a glimpse or foretaste of a universal human unity.[2]

While what is being discussed is the intimacy between an I and a Thou, here—as in Turner and Buber and, in a different way, Jung—this specific intimacy opens one to the "larger intersubjective life," to the experience of universal human unity. Living in community, be it a marriage, a family, a religious community, or whatever is a challenge. It is not only not easy; its price has sooner or later to be paid in pain. And that pain is not for the sake of "chumminess" but for the sake of finding a situation where the essential solitude and individuation process of each person is respected. Only there does one find an I, a Thou, a We. But insofar as such a dream can be realized—and there have been cases in these pages which suggest that it can—such a community in freedom becomes a sign of something for which all people yearn. Andrei Rublev's icon *The Trinity* presents God as community. Dante's *Paradiso* sees heaven in terms of harmonious unity in diversity. In the end our lives seek their balance of solitude and community. Those who by their lives can point the way in this direction are truly blessed. They show us something of Scripture's kingdom of peace.

EPILOGUE: THE MYSTERY OF COMMUNITY

In various bits of literature there is an account of people who eat with long utensils. They do not—in fact, cannot—feed themselves. They would starve if they tried. Rather, they feed each other.

In some ways the thought of being fed may hardly seem attractive, but it is about the ability to receive. However, seen from the active side, the concern to feed others can be equally important—not the false concern that expresses desire to care but without caring from the heart, not the feeling that one "ought" to care which is socialized into people. Rather, the important concern is the kind of caring that is another name for love and that respects the other's freedom, solitude, space.

In an age when popular psychology encourages us all to assertiveness and self-interest, this real concern for another person—let alone for a group living mutually in this way, living a We—can be a breath of fresh air. It is interesting that a psychology as concerned with individuation as Jung's should see the deeper reaches of this process in terms of life less controlled by and centered on ego, more attuned to the "Self" that is no longer one's single little self!

Most human beings live with others, at least during much of their lives. We grow up in a family; many of us marry or live in community. It may be that all this is training and preparation for the greater solitude of later years—which can also be a greater love. Living with others bears fruit in us—whether of bitterness or mellowing, of anguish, defensiveness, or caring, and usually a blend of all of these. Community is a training ground.

But it is also a mystery—as is any place where there is a battle between love and iniquity. Our heart is the real battleground, but what happens in our hearts emerges in our life with others. There is no heart or life without "iniquity" or the shadow. But there are people who, in the acceptance of the darkness in reality have also become bearers of light and love. There are families and communities which, knowing themselves as *"semper refor-manda"* on deep levels, also live in forgiveness and this same love. Perhaps arriving at this point is wisdom, which accepts the fallible, weak, and sinful, and transfigures it—not so that it ceases to be itself but so that there is healing. Individuation, ultimately, is in no way a question of self-aggrandizement. Rather, it is about opening to an Other, about this living relationship which in some religious circles would be called love. Community, then, is a place where one can learn about relationship and about love—a place where we are challenged to risk the suffering needed to grow in love, a suffering without which real adulthood is rarely possible. Community can also be a place where one meets not only these but also more than the merely human. Where it is lived—and even where it is badly lived—community is a place of mystery. But where people learn from and live the training it provides, it is also a place of learning to open ourselves to Love.

NOTES

Introduction

1. Charles A. Fracchia, *Living Together Alone: The New American Monasticism* (San Francisco: Harper and Row, 1979), 157.
2. Ibid.
3. Ibid., 162.
4. Ibid.

Chapter 1, "A History of Religious Community in the West"

1. Acts 2:46.
2. Acts 2:46, 4:32.
3. Cassian, "Conference XVIII (Of Abbot Piamun: Of the Three Sorts of Monks)," in vol. II of *A Select Library of Nicene and Post-Nicene Fathers of the Christian Church,* series 2, trans. Philip Schaff and Henry Wall (Grand Rapids, Mich.: Eerdmans, 1978).
4. See *The Rule of Saint Augustine,* intr. Tarcisius J. Van Bavel, OSA; trans. Raymond Canning, OSA (Garden City, N.Y.: Doubleday Image Books, 1986) (both the masculine and the feminine versions). See also Augustine's commentary on Psalm 132.
5. See *The Rule of Taizé in French and in English* (Taizé, France: Les Presses de Taizé, 1967), 136–37.
6. Benedicta Ward, trans., *The Sayings of the Desert Fathers: The Alphabetical Collection* (Kalamazoo, Mich.: Cistercian Publications, 1975), 63.
7. Ibid., 73.
8. Quoted in "Pachomius and Cenobitic Monasticism," *RB 1980: The Rule of St. Benedict in Latin and English with Notes* (Collegeville, Minn.:

Liturgical Press, 1981), 21. Quotations from the Benedictine Rule in this text henceforth referred to as *RB*.

9. Ibid., 25.

10. "The Long Rules," in *Saint Basil: Ascetical Works*, trans. Sister M. Monica Wagner, CSC, vol. 9 of *The Fathers of the Church: A New Translation*, ed. Roy Joseph Deferrari et al. (New York: Fathers of the Church, 1950), 252.

After a description of the footwashing: "Whom, therefore, will you [the hermit] wash? To whom will you minister? In comparison with whom will you be the lowest if you live alone?" (question 7).

11. *RB*, 1:6–9.

12. Ibid., 48:8.

13. Ibid., 71:1.

14. Ibid., 72:4–11.

15. See chap. 15, "Paradisus Claustralis," in Thomas Merton, *The Waters of Siloe* (New York: Harcourt Brace Jovanovich, 1979).

16. *RB*, 58:25. After profession the monk must be "well aware that from that day he will not have even his own body at his disposal."

17. Taped conference by Ambrose Wathen, OSB.

18. A good example, which does not use the word "barracks" but which the author applies to apostolic community life in general, occurs in George A. Aschenbrunner, SJ, "Active and Monastic: Two Apostolic Lifestyles," *Review for Religious* 45, no. 5 (Sept./Oct. 1986), 662–63. "In an active religious community, the members come together precisely in order to be sent out on specific ministries, each of which shares in God's mission of salvation in Jesus."

See the discussion of this question in Michael J. Buckley, SJ, "Mission in Companionship: Of Jesuit Community and Communion," *Studies in the Spirituality of Jesuits* 11, no. 4 (Sept. 1979).

19. Mary Magdalen Bellasis, OSU, *The Origins of the Roman Union to Its Foundation in 1900*, vol. 1 of *History of the Roman Union of the Order of Saint Ursula*, adapted from the French of Marie Vianney Boschet, OSU (Exeter, N.H.: Catholic Records Press, n.d.), 1.

20. Ibid., 2.

21. Ibid.

22. Ibid., 3.

23. Teresa Ledochowska, OSU, *Angela Merici and the Company of St. Ursula, According to the Historical Documents*, vol. 2 of *The Evolution of the Primitive Company*, trans. Mary Teresa Neylan, OSU (Rome: Ancora, 1967), 134.

24. See *RB*, 22:8.

25. See "Decree on the Appropriate Renewal of the Religious Life,"

in *The Documents of Vatican II,* ed. Walter M. Abbot, SJ (New York: Guild Press, 1966), 468.

26. On the whole subject of charisms of religious communities, a good study and demonstration of method is Teresa Ledochowska, OSU, *In Search of the Charism of the Institute of the Ursulines of the Roman Union,* trans. Mary Antony Lawrence, OSU, and Mary Magdalen Bellasis, OSU (privately printed in Rome, 1976).

27. See Raimundo Pannikar et al., *Blessed Simplicity: The Monk as Universal Archetype* (New York: Seabury, 1982), especially Myriam Dardenne, "Who Is the Integrating Subject? A Response from a Western Point of View," 178–94.

Chapter 2, "Community—Dead or Alive?"

1. Adolf Guggenbühl-Craig, *Marriage: Dead or Alive,* trans. Murray Stein (Dallas: Spring Publications, 1981).

2. Ibid., 26–27.

3. Ibid., 27.

4. Ibid.

5. Members of secular institutes also live a life vowed to God but they do not normally live in community.

6. Guggenbühl, 29.

7. Ibid., 30.

8. See André Louf's discussion of the whole question from the point of view of spirituality and celibacy in *Teach Us to Pray: Learning a Little about God,* trans. Hubert Hoskins (New York: Paulist, 1975), 63–68.

9. Guggenbühl, 31.

10. See I. Hausherr, SJ, *Les Leçons d'un contemplatif: Le Traité de l'oraison d'Evagre le Pontique* (Paris: Beauchesne, 1960), 187.

11. Guggenbühl, 9.

12. Ibid., 10.

13. Ibid., 112.

14. Ibid., 15.

15. Ibid.

16. Ibid., 21.

17. Ibid., 41.

18. Ibid., 42.

19. Ibid., 43.

20. John of the Cross, "Counsels to a Religious on How to Reach Perfection," in *The Collected Works of John of the Cross,* trans. Kieran Ka-

vanaugh, OCD, and Otilio Rodriguez, OCD (Washington, D.C.: ICS Publications, Institute of Carmelite Studies, 1979), n. 3.

21. *RB*, 1:2–5.
22. Guggenbühl, 46.
23. Ibid., 60–61.
24. Ibid., 61.
25. Ibid.
26. Ibid., 102–3.
27. Ibid., 103.
28. Ibid., 103–6.
29. Ibid., 109.
30. Ibid., 115.

Chapter 3, "Perseverance or Escape?"

1. John of the Cross, "The Precautions," in *Collected Works,* n. 8.

Chapter 4, "Shalom"

1. *Inflation* is a Jungian term for "exaggeration, a puffed-up attitude." See, for example, C. G. Jung, *Two Essays on Analytical Psychology,* 2nd ed., trans. R. F. C. Hull (Princeton University Press, 1966), 71.

Chapter 7, "Bed and Breakfast, or Large Community?"

1. Joan D. Chittister, OSB, *Living the Rule Today: A Series of Conferences on the Rule of Benedict* (Erie, Penn.: Benet Press, 1982), 98–99.

Chapter 9, "Exclusion or Inclusion?"

1. Jean M. Auel, *The Mammoth Hunters* (New York: Crown, 1985), 166.
2. Ibid., 170.

Chapter 10, "A Therapeutic Community"

1. Jacqui Lee Schiff with Beth Day, *All My Children* (New York: Pyramid, 1970).

2. Ibid., 38.

3. Ibid., 6–7.

4. Ibid., 25.

5. Ibid., 55.

6. Ibid., 214.

7. See "The Psychology of the Transference Interpreted in Conjunction with a Set of Alchemical Pictures," in *The Practice of Psychotherapy: Essays on the Psychology of the Transference and Other Subjects,* 2nd ed., vol. 16 of *The Collected Works of C. G. Jung,* trans. R. F. C. Hull (Princeton University Press, 1966), 261–62.

Chapter 11, "Priorities"

1. See also the excellent discussion of these subjects in chapter 4 of Robert N. Bellah et al., *Habits of the Heart: Individualism and Commitment in American Life* (New York: Harper and Row, 1985). (That I find the discussion excellent does not, of course, imply that I agree unreservedly with everything said there!)

2. M. Scott Peck, M.D., *The Road Less Travelled: A New Psychology of Love, Traditional Values and Spiritual Growth* (New York: Simon and Schuster, 1978), 54.

3. See chapter 1 of John A. Sanford, *The Invisible Partners: How the Male and Female in Each of Us Affects Our Relationships* (New York: Paulist, 1983).

4. I have not found the exact quotation. The opening paragraphs of *The Interior Castle* come close. See *The Collected Works of St. Teresa of Avila,* vol. 2, trans. Otilio Rodriguez, OCD, and Kieran Kavanaugh, OCD (Washington, D.C.: ICS Publications, Institute of Carmelite Studies, 1980).

5. Dietrich Bonhoeffer, *Life Together: A Study of Christian Fellowship,* trans. John W. Doberstein (San Francisco: Harper and Row, 1954), 77.

6. Rabindranath Tagore, *The King of the Dark Chamber* (New York: Macmillan, 1915).

Chapter 12, "Five *S*'s: Solitude, Sexuality, Space, Sharing, Stability"

1. Robert McAllister, M.D., "Characteristics of Community," *Sisters Today* 57, no. 6 (Feb. 1985), 323–35. This article appears as chapter 3 of his book *Living the Vows* (San Francisco: Harper and Row, 1985), 323.

2. Ibid., 327.

3. Ibid., 328.

4. Ibid.

5. See the explanation of these concepts and their discussion in terms of Jesuit (and possibly other active) communities in Michael J. Buckley, SJ, "Mission in Companionship: Of Jesuit Community and Communion," *Studies in the Spirituality of Jesuits* 11, no. 4 (Sept. 1979), 6–8.

6. Herbert W. Richardson, *Nun, Witch, Playmate: The Americanization of Sex* (Lewiston, N.Y.: Mellen Press, 1971), chap. 5.

7. Thomas M. King, SJ, "Even Discipline Has Its Season: Thomas Merton and Formation Today," *Review for Religious* 44, no. 6 (Nov./ Dec. 1985), 808–14.

8. Bellah, 91.

Chapter 13, "Some Anthropological Considerations"

1. Victor W. Turner, *The Ritual Process: Structure and Anti-Structure* (Chicago: Aldine, 1969).

2. Ibid., 94–130.

3. Victor and Edith Turner, *Image and Pilgrimage in Christian Culture: Anthropological Perspectives* (New York: Columbia University Press, 1978), 249.

4. Turner, *Ritual Process*, 94.

5. Ibid., 96.

6. Ibid.

7. Ibid., 97.

8. Ibid.

9. Ibid.

10. Ibid., 103.

11. Ibid., 104–5.

12. Ibid., 105.

13. Ibid.

14. Ibid., 107.

15. Ibid., 110.

16. Ibid., 111.

17. Ibid., 112.

18. Ibid., 114.

19. Ibid., 125.

20. Ibid., 126.

21. Martin Buber, *Between Man and Man*, trans. R. G. Smith (London: Fontana Library, 1961), 51. Quoted in Turner, *Ritual Process*, 127.

22. Turner, *Ritual Process*, 128.

23. Ibid.
24. Ibid., 129.
25. Ibid., 131–32.
26. Buber, 213–14. Quoted in Turner, *Ritual Process* 137.
27. Turner, 139.
28. Ibid., 146.
29. Ibid., 180.
30. Ibid., 182.
31. Ibid.
32. Ibid., 183.
33. Ibid., 185.
34. Ibid., 189.

Chapter 14, "Insights from C. G. Jung"

1. C. G. Jung, "The Psychology of the Transference Interpreted in Conjunction with a Set of Alchemical Pictures," in *The Practice of Psychotherapy: Essays on the Psychology of the Transference and Other Subjects,* 2nd ed., trans. R. F. C. Hull (Princeton University Press, 1966). References will be made to paragraphs rather than pages.
2. This is a medieval alchemical text.
3. Jung, "Transference," 416.
4. Ibid., 418.
5. Ibid., 419.
6. Jung describes transference as a projection onto the doctor of "archaic infantile fantasies which were originally vested in members of the patient's own family," 420.
7. Ibid.
8. Ibid.
9. This theme has been much discussed by Alice Miller, for example in her *Thou Shalt Not Be Aware: Society's Betrayal of the Child,* trans. Hildegarde and Hunter Hannum (New York: Farrar, Straus, and Giroux, 1984).
10. Jung, "Transference," 420.
11. Ibid.
12. Ibid., 431.
13. John Layard, "The Incest Taboo and the Virgin Archetype," *Eranos-Jahrbuch,* vol. 12 (Zurich, 1944–1945), 253ff.; Alfred William Howitt, *The Native Tribes of South-East Australia* (London, 1904); Sir James George Frazer, *Totemism and Exogamy,* 4 vols. (London, 1910).
14. Jung, "Transference," 434.
15. Ibid., 435.

16. Ibid., 438.
17. Ibid.
18. Ibid.
19. Ibid., 439.
20. Ibid., 440.
21. Ibid., 442.
22. Ibid., 443.
23. Ibid., 444.
24. Ibid., 445.
25. Ibid.
26. Ibid.

"Interlude (Playing in between)"

1. Starhawk, *Dreaming the Dark: Magic, Sex, and Politics* (Boston: Beacon Press, 1982), 78.
2. Ibid., 86.
3. Ibid., 29.
4. Ibid., 92.
5. Ibid., 96.
6. Ibid., 98.
7. Ibid., 99–100.
8. Ibid., 155.
9. Joan H. Timmerman, *The Mardi Gras Syndrome: Rethinking Christian Sexuality* (New York: Crossroad, 1986), 30.
10. Ibid., 52.
11. Ibid., 68.
12. Ibid., 75–76.
13. See above, chap. 12, note 5.
14. Sandra M. Schneiders, IHM, *New Wineskins: Re-Imagining Religious Life Today* (New York: Paulist, 1986), 106.

"Conclusions"

1. Raimundo Panikkar, *Blessed Simplicity: The Monk as Universal Archetype* (New York: Seabury, 1982), 19–20.
2. Sebastian Moore, *Let This Mind Be in You: The Quest for Identity through Oedipus to Christ* (New York: Harper and Row, 1986), 25.